ROUGH DRAFT MATH

REVISING TO LEARN

Rough Draft Math can help teachers create classroom environments where learning is seen as a process not an event. By encouraging initial or unfinished thinking, students feel safe and free to participate without fear of being wrong. By emphasizing the sharing and refining of ideas, not solely on getting the right answer, rough draft math can support each and every student in feeling valued and competent. In this book Jansen provides a resource that will help teachers ensure that all student voices are heard. A "must read" for all teachers!

—Margaret (Peg) Smith, Professor Emerita, University of Pittsburgh,
Co-Author, 5 Practices for Orchestrating Productive Mathematics Discussions

Many students think math is either right or wrong and fear that for them it's usually wrong. Amanda Jansen refocuses all of us on math's big ideas and helps us see that student understanding of those ideas is never wrong. Rather, it's always in process, always moving from one draft to the next, guided by useful teaching moves Jansen will help you learn.

—Dan Meyer, Chief Academic Officer, Desmos

I was immediately drawn to the idea of "Rough Draft Math" and the powerful potential of this work for rehumanizing mathematics, promoting equity and access, and empowering students, especially students who have not been served well (or fully centered) in mathematics classrooms. *Rough Draft Math: Revising to Learn* has the potential to dramatically improve the quality of mathematics teaching and learning for all students by opening spaces in classrooms and creating new opportunities for students to show their mathematical brilliance as it unfolds and is in progress, instead of focusing on final solutions or explanations. This book is imperative for current and future mathematics teachers, mathematics teacher educators, and administrators. In this clearly written, practical guide, Mandy Jansen leverages classroom illustrations paired with usable advice for creating or re-designing classrooms where students (and their ideas) are the center. This work involves examining and considering revisions to the classroom culture, tasks that are selected and used, as well as teaching practices that focus on students as both sense makers and valuable contributors to the mathematics learning of the class.

—Imani Goffney, Assistant Professor, University of Maryland,
Co-Editor, Rehumanizing Mathematics for Black, Indigenous, and Latinx Students

ROUGH DRAFT MATH

REVISING TO LEARN

Amanda JANSEN

Foreword by Robert Q. Berry III

Stenhouse PUBLISHERS

PORTSMOUTH, NEW HAMPSHIRE

Stenhouse Publishers
www.stenhouse.com

Credits
Figures 2.1, 2.2, 2.3, 2.4 Copyright © 2011 Mathematics Assessment Resource Service - www.map.mathshell.org.
Figure 2.7 Reprinted with permission from Mathematics Teacher Educator, copyright © 2016, by the National Council of Teachers of Mathematics. All rights reserved.
Figure 3.5 Used with permission from www.mathalicious.com.
Walkathon Task on page 61 is adapted from *Connected Mathematics Project.*
Figure 5.1 Adapted from visualpatterns.org.

Library of Congress Cataloging-in-Publication Data

Names: Jansen, Amanda, author.
Title: Rough draft math : revising to learn / Amanda Jansen.
Description: Portsmouth, New Hampshire : Stenhouse Publishers, [2020] | Includes bibliographical references and index.
Identifiers: LCCN 2019040332 (print) | LCCN 2019040333 (ebook) | ISBN 9781625312068 (paperback) | ISBN 9781625312075 (ebook)
Subjects: LCSH: Mathematics--Study and teaching. | Motivation in education. | Teacher-student relationships. | Classroom environment.
Classification: LCC QA16 .J36 2020 (print) | LCC QA16 (ebook) | DDC 510.71--dc23
LC record available at https://lccn.loc.gov/2019040332
LC ebook record available at https://lccn.loc.gov/2019040333

Cover design, interior design, and typesetting: Alessandra S. Turati; cover photograph of graph paper ©thepixel via 123RF

Printed in the United States of America
This book is printed on paper certified by third-party standards for sustainably managed forestry.

27 26 25 24 23 22 21 4371 8 7 6 5 4 3 2

I dedicate this book to my niece,
Katherine Amanda Ellersick

What the best and wisest parent wants for his own child, that must the community want for all of its children.

—John Dewey, *The School and Society*

contents

foreword

I first learned about rough draft talk at a conference presentation from Mandy Jansen and her colleagues. From this presentation, I situated rough draft talk as an equitable instructional routine allowing students to share thinking in a way that positioned them as mathematically competent by allowing them to share their thinking while their ideas might be still under construction. When I read Jansen's and her colleagues' article "Rough-Draft Talk in Mathematics Classrooms" published in *Mathematics Teaching in the Middle School* (2017), it provided me a deeper understanding of how she connected rough draft talk with equitable instructional practices. I have since used rough draft talk as an instructional practice for the students I teach at my university and the middle school boys I taught in the summers. I wanted my students to have space where their voices are heard, feel a sense of security if they felt participation was risk-taking, and know that they are mathematically competent. Rough draft talk allows me to take risks when I am uncertain about my thinking. I often engage in rough draft talk with students (and colleagues) when I need to voice my thoughts about mathematical ideas. Sometimes I say, "My ideas are not fully conceptualized, but here is what I am thinking." Similarly, by valuing my students' willingness to participate and share their mathematical ideas, having or not having fully developed mathematical ideas are acceptable in our spaces. Rough draft thinking and talk help me position each and every student as being mathematically competent.

I believe that each and every student is mathematically competent and can learn high-level mathematics and that equitable, intentional teaching opens up interactional space for a broad range of teaching and learning ideas. *Rough Draft Math* can help teachers position students as mathematically competent and support mathematical identity and agency in a number of ways, such as the following:

- promoting mathematical discourse
- establishing and upholding structures such as norms and routines that provide opportunities for all students to engage in that discourse
- shifting students' views of competence from performative to participatory
- developing students' intellectual authority
- positioning students as sensemakers by sharing that intellectual authority
- focusing on mathematical goals and conceptual understanding
- encouraging risk-taking
- building active, nurturing, and collegial communities in which students feel a sense of inclusion and belonging

Promoting and valuing students' participation in mathematical discourse is a way of positioning students as mathematically competent. Mathematical discourse includes but is not limited to students engaged in deep mathematical thinking; sharing their reasoning, creating and revising their thinking; and engaging in collaborations aimed at making sense of and using mathematical ideas. To ensure that each and every student not only understands and can make use of mathematics concepts and relationships but also comes to experience the joy, wonder, and beauty of mathematics, we must position each and every student as mathematically competent. If we consider mathematical competence as being the ways in which students participate in mathematics, then this book provides the framing for mathematical competence as participation through talk, thinking, and connecting with others.

Building mathematical competency requires creating classroom structures—norms and routines—that support students to take risks to engage in discourse and to see themselves as capable and worthy of being heard.

Mathematical discourse includes not only participating in mathematics talk but also having one's ideas be heard. Those who talk and are listened to in mathematical discourse are positioned as mathematically competent. We must provide opportunities for each and every student to talk and to have their ideas heard during mathematics classrooms. Chapter 2 of this book focuses on building a culture of rough draft thinking such that teachers can create classroom structures and norm in which students can make their mathematical ideas public.

I have observed too many mathematics classrooms positioning mathematical competence solely based on quickness and correctness of mathematical solutions, ideas, and thinking, giving the mistaken impression that only some students are "good at math." This creates an environment where students' mathematical reasoning goes unexamined and unvalued; consequently, little is known about how they make sense of mathematics, how they use their mathematical understanding in developing solutions, and why their solutions do or do not make sense. Correct answers matter but not as indicators of who can do mathematics. Throughout this book, Jansen positions rough draft thinking and talk as instructional practices supportive of engaging in mathematical discourse, which is essential for developing a mathematical identity. Specifically, Chapter 5 discusses rough draft thinking as a rehumanizing approach, valuing connections among students and teachers.

When students share and value their mathematical ideas through mathematical discourse, they move away from mathematics competence as producing correct answers quickly and toward mathematics competence as participatory. Aguirre, Mayfield-Ingram, and Martin (2013) define mathematical identity as "the dispositions and deeply held beliefs that students develop about their ability to participate and perform effectively in mathematical contexts and to use mathematics in powerful ways across the contexts of their lives" (14). The power I find in this definition of mathematical identity is the connection to being participatory and performance. That is, participation and performance are connected to practices and processes for doing mathematics. I believe that students' mathematics identity is closely associated with whether and how they have opportunities to talk, listen, and be heard using their mathematical ideas. Consequently, classroom structures and instructional routines can either create or limit opportunities for positioning students as mathematically competent. Rough draft thinking and talk are intentional, instructional acts supportive of positioning students as mathematically competent and developing positive mathematical identity.

As students author ideas, decide and justify whether particular ideas are reasonable, and press one another for explanations, they take on forms of intellectual authority that support collaborative mathematics teaching and learning. Students, as sense-makers, require opportunities to construct their ideas through reflection, refining, and extending prior ideas, knowledge, and experiences. The ideas in *Rough Draft Math* help us see how to position students as sense-makers because authority is shared between students and teachers. That is, not all mathematical ideas are authored primarily by teachers, and students have the autonomy to author and share their ideas. For many teachers, positioning students as sense-makers can feel like risk-taking because they may not feel like they are controlling the narrative. That is, some teachers may think ideas must be authored by teachers and presented as correct, concise, and clean rather than authored by students as rough, then refined, and revoiced. The stories in this book can help us revise our own thinking about ideas in the mathematics classroom and see that positioning students as sense-makers and sharing authority in mathematics classrooms create the space for students to see themselves and others as mathematically competent while developing conceptual understanding.

The presence of talk in mathematics lessons is necessary but not sufficient to promote deeper learning. Talking and listening are critical first steps toward fostering mathematical discourse, where the teacher must pose purposeful questions, elicit student thinking, and facilitate meaningful discourse (NCTM 2014). Teachers must find a balance between allowing students to express thinking freely while keeping the focus on the mathematical learning goal(s). Mathematical discourse is a multidimensional practice where students and the teacher share ideas, questions, and other mathematical wonderings to build mathematical understanding. Jansen's examples and analysis provide rich opportunities for readers to reflect on the complex practice of facilitating discourse in service of mathematical goals.

For many students, participation in mathematics classrooms is risk-taking. The feeling of risk-taking might be that in many mathematics classrooms, quickness and correctness of mathematical solutions are valued more than providing students opportunities to evolve in the development of their mathematical ideas and recognizing that their ideas are worthy of being heard, even if unfinished. In contrast, rough draft thinking and talk support risk-taking, as well as create the space and a sense of safety for students (and teachers) to evolve in the development of their mathematical ideas.

Building a positive learning community in the mathematics classroom is vital. Rough draft thinking and talk contribute to this sense of community because all people are active participants through the relationships and interdependence developed for authoring and sharing ideas. Students and teachers collaborate to think, persevere, and refine ideas. Communities are intentionally active, nurturing, and collegial such that members feel a sense of inclusion. Through rough draft thinking and talk, teachers and students are building knowledge together rather competing for answers. That is, this book provides us with the framework for developing inclusive spaces for connecting mathematical ideas, knowledge generation, and positioning each and every student as worthy of being heard and seen.

Robert Q. Berry III
NCTM President (2018–2020)
Samuel Braley Gray Professor of Mathematics Education,
University of Virginia

acknowledgments

It's hard to say when the process of writing a book begins. I would not have known about the power of rough draft thinking without the scholarship of Douglas Barnes. His work on exploratory talk resonated with me so much. I could not let go of it from the first time I read about the idea, back in graduate school. It is my dream for mathematics classrooms to shift from spaces where students feel like they need to perform to places where they explore.

I began working on my understanding of rough draft thinking in earnest when Jamila Riser, director of the Delaware Mathematics Coalition, provided the space and time for me to learn by inviting me to develop an exploratory talk study group with secondary mathematics teachers from across Delaware in the spring of 2016. My own learning was enriched because of the thinking shared by teachers in our study group: Brandy Cooper, Stefanie Vascellaro, Phil Wandless, Kathleen Wilson, Debbie Tuson, and Michael Reitemeyer, among others. I have fond memories of our study group semester together, and I feel a deep sense of gratitude for how these colleagues engaged in months of sustained thinking and learning with me. At that time, I certainly did not realize that the ideas we all worked on together would grow into a book. Brandy, Stef, and Phil collaborated with me to write an article in *Mathematics Teaching in the Middle School* that we titled "Rough-Draft Talk in Mathematics Classrooms." Now, I think about that article like a preview trailer for a film, and this book is like the full-length movie.

My learning with and from Delaware teachers has continued in regular meetings of a summer professional learning community. I have been one of the cofacilitators of a problem-based learning academy for secondary teachers in Lewes, Delaware. We fondly call this learning academy Delaware Math Camp. Rough draft thinking has been a theme that we have continued to integrate into our work during Delaware Math Camp each year. I have appreciated how the other cofacilitators (Tom Becker, Robin Corrozi, Michael Reitemeyer, and Jamila Riser) have helped me see how they apply the ideas of rough draft thinking into their own teaching of adult learners—other mathematics teachers. The teachers who have attended our math camps also push my thinking when I hear about how they have worked on creating rough draft spaces in their own classrooms, including Molly Brnich, Suzi Sappington, and Shellee Wong. It is a privilege to work in an ongoing way with other mathematics teachers and teacher leaders in Delaware, and I'm so thankful that they want to think with me about rough drafts in math classrooms. I learn so much from everyone who participates in Delaware Math Camp.

I also want to express gratitude for the Teachers Development Group in West Linn, Oregon. Linda Foreman (founder and former CEO of TDG) and Ruth Heaton (current CEO of TDG) have given me space and time to work on ideas about rough draft thinking on a yearly basis at their annual leadership seminar since 2015. The opportunity to interact each year with attendees at the leadership seminar, with other speakers, and with the TDG staff is consistently a productive time for my own learning and growth. Speakers are challenged to bring their in-progress ideas and delve deeply into them with seminar attendees, and so each year at the TDG Leadership Seminar, the ideas for this book continued to develop. Since joining the TDG board of directors in 2016, I have found strong encouragement for working on rough draft thinking from other board members. When Peg Smith was on the TDG board, she saw the potential of the idea of rough draft thinking, which encouraged me to continue to develop the ideas. I wouldn't have been motivated to write the *Mathematics Teaching in the Middle School* article if another TDG board member, Cathy Martin, hadn't asked me repeatedly for an article to share with teachers about rough draft thinking. I'm thankful for the TDG community, and this book would not be the same without my experiences with those whom I had chances to interact with at the leadership seminars.

Eva Thanheiser helped me see that rough draft thinking was worth exploring through writing. She and I conducted a study together about rough draft thinking in her mathematics content course for future teachers at Portland State University, and we published it in the *Mathematics Teacher Educator* titled, "Inviting Prospective Teachers to Share Rough Draft

Mathematical Thinking." Without her, I don't know whether I would have started this line of work in the first place.

I appreciate conversations I have had with Imani Goffney about cautious points during the implementation of rough draft thinking. Imani helped me realize that we should pay attention to which students are being positioned as having rough ideas. She has been a helpful thought partner as I think through equity issues and rough draft thinking.

Thank you to Allison Gantt, a middle school mathematics teacher in Delaware, for providing insightful feedback on Chapter 3 of this book.

The mathematics teachers and educators on Twitter are one of my professional learning communities. I am grateful that so many folks on Twitter have responded to the idea of rough draft thinking. I gain inspiration from #MTBoS (Math Twitter Blog-o-Sphere) and #iteachmath on Twitter on a regular basis.

Thank you to my friend Robert Berry for his willingness to read this book in advance and write the foreword. I am inspired by his work to amplify the brilliance of Black boys doing mathematics. I appreciate his generosity in supporting this work during some of his presentations as the president of the National Council of Teachers of Mathematics.

It would not be an understatement, however, to say that this book would not have happened at all if Tracy Zager did not see the potential for the ideas to be rich enough to become a book. Before exploring the idea for this book with Tracy, I thought that I was probably done with writing about rough draft thinking after writing the journal article. But Tracy nudged me to think about whether I had more to say, and she helped me see that a book could be a space to honor what I have learned from other teachers about creating rough draft learning spaces.

As this book's editor, Tracy has read multiple early drafts of every chapter. Through Tracy, I have learned firsthand what it means to see strengths in another person's work and help the thinker continue to grow in ways that build on those strengths. She would point out where my voice and ideas were clearer and more readable and then help me see how I would be able to use that approach to improve other chapter sections. Through her feedback to writers, she models how I strive to be as a teacher; she supported my learning by challenging me to grow while still nurturing my voice. She helped me write a much better version of what I wanted to write. This book is so much better because Tracy was its first reader.

I'm thankful as well for everyone at Stenhouse. I'm humbled and honored to be a Stenhouse author, for this group is like a family who believes in its members. They hold one another up. The Stenhouse team trusted me when I needed more time to write than I originally planned. Specifically, I'd like to thank Stephanie Levy and Shannon St. Peter. Thanks go out as well to everyone in Production, Marketing, and Customer Service at Stenhouse.

I appreciate the support and patience of the people in my life—Joan, Laura, Amy, and Charles. They listened, they encouraged me, they gave me space when I needed it, and they believed in me. I'm lucky to have them on my team. I can only hope to be as supportive to them as they are to me.

I have viewed the process of writing this book as an act of curation. I wanted to document and curate what I have learned about how mathematics teachers use rough drafts in their classrooms. I would have not been able to write this book if other mathematics teachers had not been willing to try to use rough drafts in their classrooms and to share their experiences with me. Rough draft thinking has been a generative idea. Because there is no one single way to enact rough draft thinking, every time I hear about what another teacher has tried, in the spirit of rough drafting, I keep learning. I appreciate that teachers have shared with me how the idea of rough drafts have made it into their mathematics classrooms, particularly through our interactions on Twitter and at conferences.

Ending this book is hard for me. My thinking has evolved so much since I started writing it. It's almost ironic to me to have a book about rough draft thinking published in what looks like a final draft form. But the biggest reason why this book is difficult to finish is because writing about these ideas has been a joyful experience. I have kept learning and growing as I wrote and revised. I don't want the process to end. However, my learning process to improve my teaching won't ever end. I can view this book as preserving my thinking about rough drafts in math class at this point in time. I hope that my opportunities to dialogue with others about rough draft thinking will continue so we can all keep growing together.

a note to readers

My name is Mandy Jansen, and being a math teacher is an important part of who I am. Earlier in my career, I taught junior high mathematics. Now I teach future elementary and middle school teachers to help them develop a deeper understanding of mathematics for teaching, children's thinking about mathematics, and pedagogical approaches for teaching mathematics. I also teach graduate students about conducting research in education. I conduct professional development for practicing teachers throughout the state of Delaware and elsewhere at the secondary level.

Formally, I am Dr. Amanda Jansen, a professor at the University of Delaware in the School of Education with a joint appointment in the Department of Mathematical Sciences. Prior to earning my PhD in Educational Psychology at Michigan State University, I taught in Mesa, Arizona. My undergraduate degree is in mathematics with a secondary teaching certification and a minor in English from the University of Arizona.

I orient myself as an ongoing learner about teaching, and my intention in this book is to share what I have learned from collaborating with classroom teachers. Most of the teachers represented in these chapters are teachers in Delaware with whom I have had ongoing interactions over a period of years. In addition, I met a few of the teachers in these chapters when I presented at the National Council of Supervisors of Mathematics, and we continued to correspond beyond the conference. I have preserved what I have learned so far about rough draft math in this book as an act of curation.

The classroom examples in these chapters are from secondary classrooms and upper elementary classrooms (grades four through twelve). I also provide some elementary mathematics content examples in my excerpts of my own teaching of future elementary school teachers. This book is targeted most directly at grades four through ten, but I have come to believe that every learning experience benefits from a rough draft approach. I hope that teachers of other grade levels, from elementary grades to those who teach adults, might also take something away from this book. (If you want to share responses to this book, please use the hashtag #RoughDraftMath on Twitter. I'm @MandyMathEd.)

All of the teachers in this book are represented by their actual names. The school names are the actual names of the schools where they worked when I gathered the data for this book. All students' names are pseudonyms. If a teacher was included in a chapter, I shared a draft of that chapter with that teacher prior to submitting the book for publication. I incorporated any feedback they shared about the chapter. I am grateful to Michael Reitemeyer, Phil Wandless, Brandy Cooper, Christine Hubbard, Siobahn Suppa, Katrina Lindo, Eli Tinkelman, Stefanie Vascellaro, Molly Brnich, Michael Sanchez, Nicole Crawford, Kathleen Wilson, Tom Stricklin, Suzi Sappington, Tom Becker, Shellee Wong, and Carla Hood for trusting me to publicly present and reflect on their teaching practice in this book. Without them, this book would not have been possible.

CHAPTER ONE

ROUGH DRAFT THINKING IN MATHEMATICS CLASSROOMS

> If I don't understand things, I'm not going to raise my hand and blurt out an answer. I think one big problem with me is that I'm afraid that the answer's wrong. I don't want to be embarrassed by having a wrong answer. That's why sometimes people don't involve themselves in the discussions.
>
> —Marissa, seventh grade

We relate to Marissa. Most of us have experienced mathematics classrooms where the "smart" students were those who arrived at correct answers quickly. If we were not sure whether our thinking was correct, we avoided sharing aloud. Everyone wants to feel smart, and no one wants to feel embarrassed for being wrong.

> Miss Cooper lets us express ourselves. And she's a fun person to do math with because there's always different ways to do the math problem and express ourselves with it. That's just a great way to help with math.
>
> —Anna, sixth grade

Anna's experience sounds like it was very different from Marissa's. Self-expression and math class went together for Anna. As she learned different ways of doing a problem, she also shared *who* she is and *how* she thinks, in ways that made sense to her. Her identity developed as her thinking about math developed. By expressing ourselves, we learn more—both about the world and about ourselves.

> And when you have to do problems, don't just sit there. You have to get into the conversation in order to actually get it yourself and make you understand it, don't just understand it like how other kids do it.
>
> —Becky, seventh grade

Communicating helped Becky develop her understanding. She did not want to sit back and absorb the thinking of others. She wanted to "get into the conversation" because that helped her understand. For Becky, communicating about her thinking supported her learning.

I have interviewed many people about what it feels like to participate in discussions during math class, from middle school students (Jansen 2006, 2008, 2012) to high school students (Jansen, Herbel-Eisenmann, and Smith 2012) to even adults (Jansen 2009). Many people want to avoid sharing their thinking unless they are sure it is correct and complete. They see math class the way Marissa does, as a place where they try to either demonstrate correct performance or avoid incorrect performance (Ames 1992; Dweck and Leggett 1988). Marissa seems to think about participating in math class as *performing*.

Anna and Becky hold an alternative view: participating during mathematics class is an opportunity to continue learning, not an obligation to perform what we already know. As we communicate, our ideas are used to reflect, to hear ourselves think, to get feedback from others, and to make sense of our ideas through reflecting on what we heard ourselves say or write. We share our thinking and grow our ideas through communicating.

The more I listened, the more I wondered what we can do to foster mathematics classroom cultures where everyone continues learning together through sharing thinking. What roles should we invite students to take on, and what opportunities should we offer? What tasks should we enact, and how should we enact them? If we want students to communicate to learn rather than to perform, what shifts and changes can we make in our mathematics classrooms?

What Is Rough Draft Thinking?

I decided to work collaboratively with secondary teachers on this inquiry, and this book reflects much of what we have learned together. We explored the idea of what Douglas Barnes has described as *exploratory talk*—using talk to "work on understanding" or talking to learn (2008, 3). We shifted the terminology from *exploratory talk* to *rough draft* talk, because rough drafts were familiar to students from language arts. As we thought and discussed together, we developed this definition of rough draft thinking:

Rough draft thinking happens when students share their unfinished, in-progress ideas and remain open to revising those ideas.

Rough drafts in mathematics go beyond *talking to learn* to include *writing to learn* (Newell 2006) or drawing pictures of our thinking to learn. Shifting the classroom culture toward communicating to learn puts students in the role of sense-makers.

Learning is a messy business. When we learn, we actively work to make sense of an idea that does not make sense to us yet. We try on new ideas by attempting to find words, symbols, or drawings to represent these ideas, either through communicating with others or through communicating with ourselves. When we talk out loud, our rough drafts can sound bumpy, with starts and stops, awkward pauses, and expressions of uncertainty (Barnes 2008). However, if I say something imperfect, that does not mean that I am flawed as a person. No one wants to be defined by how we communicate in a particular moment.

After all, expressing words informally as we try on a new idea is a sign of knowledge in transition! Communicating awkwardly as we try to make sense of things is a sign that learning is taking place. Our use of bumpy language is actually productive struggle in action. Our brains are working overtime, trying to make new connections, so we are not able to use our minds to come up with ideal ways to explain what we're thinking (Perry and Lewis 1999). We all use informal or awkward phrasing when we puzzle through something new and try to figure out whether something makes sense to us.

Our thinking constantly evolves. We can view participating in mathematics class as sharing our current ideas—our rough drafts—as they are, while they are in progress. Ideas can be viewed as malleable, growing, ever changing, just as we are all ever changing as people. Embrace awkward ways of trying to communicate new ideas as an essential process of developing our understanding. We do not have to view awkward use of language as a flaw or a problem; it's a normal part of the process of making sense of something new. Learners can gradually shift their use of language to become more aligned with formal language use in mathematics, but they can do so when formal terminology makes sense to them.

Doing mathematics becomes more exploratory and playful when learners are open to sharing their rough draft thinking. We see these rough drafts happen when students extend their thinking and push ideas forward as they communicate. Rough drafts feel like brainstorming, testing the waters, asking questions, and sharing impressions. Rough draft thinking sounds like communicating what we notice, explaining why something does or does not seem to make sense initially, trying on a new way of seeing a relationship, or making new connections and articulating them. Learners shift into the role of explorers and feel the freedom of wondering and expressing curiosities in math class when they use rough draft thinking. They are concerned with sorting out their own thoughts rather than performing for an audience (Barnes 2008).

Experiencing Rough Draft Math

Number string used during a number talk with future elementary teachers:

$90 - 79 = ?$

$90 - 74 = ?$

$90 - 49 = ?$

$90 - 44 = ?$

Use mental math to solve each number sentence in a way that makes sense to you. How can your solution from the previous number sentence help you solve the next number sentence?

For an example of rough draft thinking in action, let me take you into my classroom, where I teach undergraduates studying to be elementary teachers at the University of Delaware in Newark, Delaware. On this day, I led the teacher candidates through a two-digit subtraction Number Talk (Humphreys and Parker 2015) involving a series of problems in a number string (see box). When we work with number strings, we start with the first problem and then reveal related problems later, one at a time, as we are ready. The previous problem in the string provides inspiration for how to think about the next problem. When I introduced the second problem (90 – 74 = ?), I encouraged my students to use mental math strategies that they had heard their colleagues use on the previous problem (90 – 79 = ?).

I challenged the teacher candidates to conceptualize subtraction as the distance between two numbers, in contrast to a removal process for subtraction, including visualizing the distance on a number line. I also nudged the teacher candidates to work on shifting the numbers from the problem on the number line to make the problem easier to solve mentally (such as shifting 90 – 79 each up one number to change the problem to 91 – 80 = ?). They knew the correct answer, but I asked them to play with strategies for finding the answer mentally. One teacher candidate took a risk to share an attempt at a strategy that was unfamiliar to her for mentally solving 90 – 74 = ?

Cara: *Shifting the number line had me all types of confused at first.*

Mandy: *Feeling all sorts of ways.*

Cara: *I did 90 – 75 in my head and got 15. Since I added 1 to the 74, I had to add to . . . I had to add another 1? See? I don't know?*

(Other teacher candidates laugh sympathetically, relating to her confusion. The question on the floor is how to handle the additional 1. Do they subtract it from the 15 to get an answer of 14 or add it to the 15 to get an answer of 16?)

Cara: *I don't like this one.*

Mandy: *So, it's like, now what do I do?*

Cara: *Yeah, I don't like this one.*

Mandy: *What about a number line?*

Cara: *Maybe. I don't know.*

Mandy: *Who wants to back this up? How was Cara thinking in a productive way that would help her get the answer?*

Beth: *This is similar to what I struggled with, with Angela's. Again, thinking, do I add or do I subtract? If you started with 75, and then from 75 to 90 is 15, then that 74 to 75 is 1. Add them together. You get 16.* (Beth draws a number line [Figure 1.1] to show the distance here.)

Just to clarify, I am not sharing this excerpt as an example of an ideal discussion. For instance, I would have loved it if I had invited Cara to share whether Beth's approach made sense to her, but I did not think to follow up in the moment. In this book, I hope readers are willing to embrace the idea that the examples have something to offer without being perfect. I would rather share real examples than ideal examples.

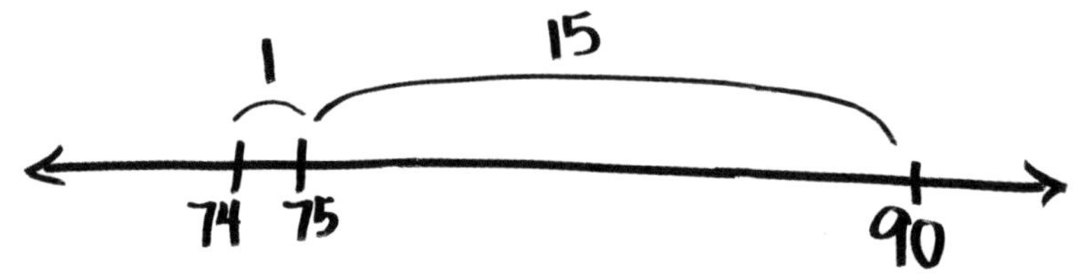

Figure 1.1
Number line illustrating the distance between 74 and 90

So, when was rough draft thinking taking place? We heard Cara take a risk and try to think about subtraction in a way that was not immediately clear to her. She tried on a strategy of adjusting the problem to make it easier to solve mentally. Cara shared her initial ideas and revised them so they become less rough. We can see that her ideas are in transition, or in rough draft states, by the false starts ("Since I added 1 to the 74, I had to add to . . . I had to add another 1?") and expressions of uncertainty ("See? I don't know."). Maybe she knew from recalled facts that 75 was 15 less than 90 and changed the problem to use that information. But then she admitted that she was not sure how to proceed from there.

I was pleased that Cara felt safe to try on a new approach, communicate her thinking about it, and admit that she was unsure about her solution. I was also pleased that her classmates were supportive and helped Cara revise her rough draft thinking. When Beth tried to make sense of Cara's thinking and build on it, she admitted that this way of thinking was hard for her at first, too. Beth tried to use a visual to help communicate and make sense of the mathematical relationships in the problem. The conversation refined and extended Cara's initial thinking. I conjecture that the entire class learned more about subtraction because Cara shared her uncertainty.

An exploratory way of engaging with mathematics also occurred in the following example, this time from Michael Reitemeyer's classroom. Mike is currently a supervisor of mathematics teachers, and he used to teach at John Dickinson High School in Wilmington, Delaware, using the *Interactive Mathematics Program* curriculum materials. Mike shared his definition of rough draft math with me: "When students put forth an unfinished idea concerned with mathematics towards peers (group or whole class) orally or in writing."

In Mike's ninth-grade inclusion classroom, he captured and documented instances of rough draft math. Here is an instance from an exponents lesson:

> In my class, students were putting out ideas like, "What do you think would happen if the base was negative?"
>
> I responded to them by saying, "Can the base be negative? How would that make sense in terms of Alice [the context for which they were attempting to learn about exponents]?"
>
> And rather than ask their groupmates simply if they were correct, students would say things like, "Hey, I got here, then tried square rooting. I don't know. That's the only thing I can think of to take out an exponent. Do you have any ideas?"
>
> —Michael Reitemeyer, Supervisor of Mathematics

In Mike's class, the students and their teacher wondered together. Students expressed curiosities, shared thinking before they were sure, and pushed one another to grow. I particularly appreciated how Mike's response to his students pushed them to continue making sense of the ideas. He did not position himself as the authority in the classroom, but instead, he transferred authority for making meaning of mathematics to the students.

Three Features of Rough Draft Math

Rough draft math is . . .

1. **Imperfect but precise.**
2. **Unfinished and unsure.**
3. **Involves revisiting and revising.**

Both of these classroom excerpts—from my and Mike's classes—illustrate that rough draft math has three important features:

1. **Imperfect but precise.** It is useful for students to use language that makes sense to them. Their efforts to communicate illuminate how students are thinking, even if the language is not mathematically perfect. A degree of precision is present when we understand each other. Rough draft math invites students to use their own ways of communicating to explore mathematics.

Children regularly use language that makes sense to them in ways that give us precise access to their thinking. Christine Newell, an elementary mathematics specialist, spoke about this idea at the 2017 annual meeting of the National Council of Supervisors of Mathematics. In this talk, she shared her son's words. He asked for "two slices of hot bread with the cheese of America." Her son may not have used the words we expected, but he used the words that made sense to him, and Christine knew he wanted a grilled cheese sandwich. His language was precise because he clearly communicated his request. We also see precise but imperfect language in the example from Mike's classroom, when a student said they "tried square rooting." Although "square rooting" is not in the formal mathematics lexicon, we know what the student meant. Promoting rough draft math in classrooms invites learners to share their thinking in their own words to explore ideas and make new connections. We can work with learners over time to refine their language, but opportunities for learners to use language that makes sense to them is a part of opening up spaces for communicating to learn.

2. **Unfinished and unsure.** When someone communicates slightly before they might feel ready, but they take the risk to put it out there, that's engaging in rough draft math. When I facilitate whole-group discussions and participants take intellectual risks bravely, I regularly hear disclaimers like, "I don't have the words yet, but . . . " or "My brain is mushy about this right now, but . . ." Indeed, I make these disclaimers myself! It's hard to get the words out when we don't know yet, but trying to communicate helps us understand more.

We heard this sort of uncertainty in the example from my classroom. Cara tried to talk through a strategy, and then she stopped and said, "See? I don't know?" By putting our uncertainties into a public space, through writing or talking, we can help one another resolve them. Uncertainty is a normal part of learning anything new, so rough draft math is an opportunity to be explicit with ourselves and with one another in order to grow.

3. **Involves revisiting and revising.** When we learn something new, our thinking evolves. Changing our thinking is more than correcting a mistake or an error. Revising our thinking can be seeing something in a new way, taking an alternative approach, making a new connection, or elaborating on our thinking to add additional insights. Rough draft math is when people purposefully remain open to shifting their thinking.

Opportunities to revisit and revise thinking can happen regularly during mathematics lessons, either spontaneously or explicitly built into the lesson. In the previous example from my classroom, I explicitly invited the teacher candidates to revise their thinking by suggesting a strategy that some of the teacher candidates had not yet tried. They took the risk of revising their thinking by attempting to see subtraction in a new way through an alternative strategy. In Mike's classroom example, the student asked for input to help revise his thinking ("That's the only thing I can think of . . . Do you have any ideas?"). We can also see revisions happening when people correct themselves, such as when they catch themselves making a mistake or when they try to see a situation in a new way.

Rough drafts, then, are not just for language arts! Let's invite and welcome opportunities to revise in mathematics class. We can use rough drafts in any situation when we want to continue to learn more through sharing initial ways of thinking. Our audiences for rough drafts can be ourselves, our peers, and our teachers. These audiences can work with us to help our rough drafts become less rough. When we use the tag *rough draft thinking*, students take it up readily because students have prior experiences with rough drafts in language arts. Students quickly start tagging their own contributions and say, "This is just my rough draft, but . . ."

Take Time to Understand Mathematics Incrementally

Bringing rough drafts into mathematics class has put the subject matter into perspective in a new way for me. When teachers ask students to share their rough draft thinking, they also ask students to revise their thinking incrementally. This is quite different from learning to obtain an answer more efficiently. Mathematics is commonly viewed as black and white, correct or incorrect. Rough draft thinking puts into perspective that, in the mathematics classroom, all learners, including the teacher, are trying to make sense of ideas over time. Students in classrooms that incorporate rough draft thinking experience learning mathematics as a process of constantly extending, connecting, and adjusting thinking.

Understanding something new takes time. I am reminded of Susan Jo Russell's notion of *productive lingering* in mathematics classrooms, which is something I have heard her share at various conferences. She talks about the power of allowing learners to dwell on various representations from a variety of perspectives over an extended period of time to deepen their understandings of important concepts, such as the behaviors of operations.

Maybe it is possible at times to bring slowed-down moments into mathematics class. Carl Honoré (2004) wrote a book called *In Praise of Slowness*. (For those of us who, ironically enough, do not have time to read this book, he gave a TED talk about the ideas [Honoré 2005]. At 10:40 into the presentation, he talks about how children, not only adults, would benefit from slowing down.) In his book, he critiqued a culture of valuing speed and instant gratification. He presents the alternative of a slower pace, which brings more pleasure, more insight, and greater connections. This means taking the time to look at a problem from many angles.

Much of our histories with mathematics classrooms likely involved speed. Who among us does not have a memory of math class that includes timed tests, mad minutes, or completing a worksheet of math facts as fast as possible? However, understanding why those facts make sense is a process on its own timetable. Slowness has a role to play in sense-making in mathematics so that students can make greater connections to and among the content, gain more insight, and take greater pleasure in thinking about mathematics. It takes time to communicate our rough draft thinking, put it out there, have the chance to revise it, and revisit the ideas. There are no shortcuts to developing our understandings.

Phil Wandless, an eighth-grade teacher in Smyrna, Delaware, reflected on how to mirror our processes of learning outside of school in classrooms.

> I think of exploratory talk as conversations we have with ourselves, but now aloud. I think we do this naturally outside of school, and it's possible that old-school instruction taught us not to use this natural skill—exploring our ideas aloud. At home, haven't you ever had someone ask you, "Who are you talking to?" In fact, you were simply thinking out loud about something that you were trying to figure out. Or maybe you heard one of your family members doing this?
>
> Then, when we went to school, I remember straight rows and no talking unless you were called on. If you were called on, you'd better have a final idea that you are no longer trying to figure out and be confident it's one hundred percent correct.
>
> Rough draft talking is not something we naturally do in front of other people, due to the thought of sounding incompetent, but what an awesome way to learn. It allows students to try out their ideas, change them as they hear it. They will have dead ends, broken sentences, and hesitation. When students first experience this, I notice that they stop talking and say something like, "I know what I want to say, but I'm not sure how to put in words."
>
> —Phil Wandless, middle school math teacher

What Does It Mean to Be Good at Math? Who Gets to Be Seen as Good at Math?

When we promote rough draft thinking, we can amplify how in-progress thinking furthers the group's mathematical understandings. In classrooms, students have perceptions about one another. Who is smart? Who is not? Teachers can disrupt these perceptions—hierarchies of academic competence (Cohen and Lotan 2014)—among students by pointing out the value of rough drafts. Sharing rough draft ideas can be a way of being good at math, because emerging thoughts can help everyone move their thinking forward.

When Phil Wandless taught eighth grade, he wanted to help students see the value of one another's rough draft thinking. He reflected with me about a video of one of his lessons. In this lesson, he asked his students to graph a story problem about a cyclist on a hill. He wanted his students to represent the rate of change on a qualitative graph of speed versus time, and he conjectured that initially students would think about the graph in terms of position at a point in time. He said, "When students first think about showing this on a speed-versus-time graph, they like to draw the elevation versus time, being confused that riding uphill would actually show a line going down on a speed versus a time graph, as your speed would decrease as you are pedaling uphill. It's a nice informal way to start understanding motion graphs and recognizing there is a change in rate at points." Phil's awareness of his students' incoming ideas helps him understand and talk with students about their in-progress thinking.

Phil introduced the lesson to me like this:

> You will notice [in this episode] that Joey is very brave. I noticed he was struggling to make sense of this math event, so I urged him to tell the class out loud what he was thinking and struggling with. This was our first day of describing nonlinear graphs when dealing with motion. Jennifer, one of the students, came to the board to share the graph she drew from a description that was given. The given information was a situation about riding a bike at a constant speed, then going up a hill, then riding down the hill.

Jennifer drew her graph well and described her thoughts to the class, but she was not thorough enough in her explanation, which left some students still puzzled. I asked them to talk to each other to restate or paraphrase what Jennifer had said, and I noticed Joey was still struggling with the concept.

—Phil Wandless

Specifically, Joey wondered about the point of inflection, as indicated by the arrow in Figure 1.2. Because Phil thought that Joey's question was powerful and worth considering, he asked Joey to talk about his in-progress thinking.

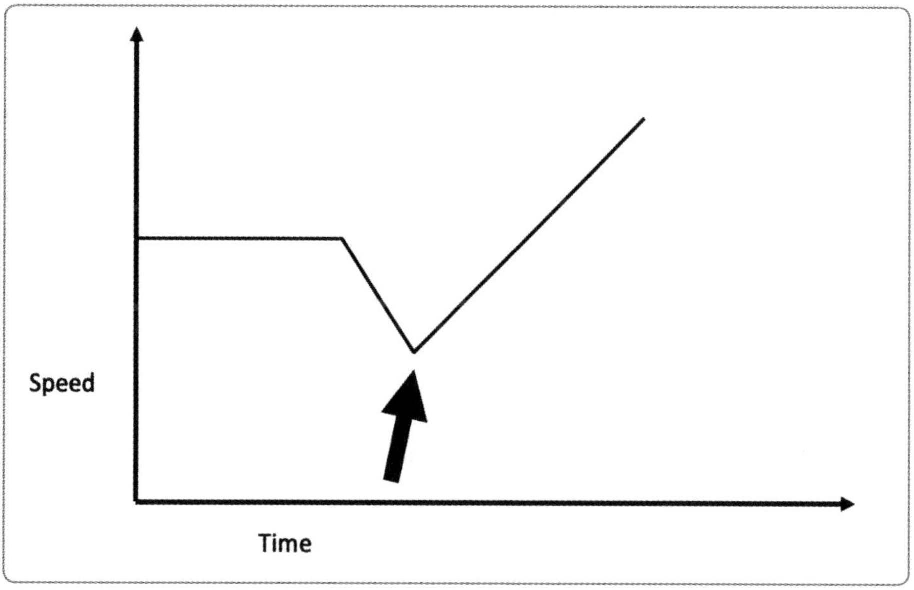

Figure 1.2
Jennifer's graph and the point in question

Joey: *You're on your way up, but the straight line is above the top of the hill. You can't start on the top of the hill if you're going up*. (Joey gestures by making an uphill motion with his hand.)

Phil: *Can anyone answer that?*

Sarah: *What did he say?*

Phil: *Say it again a little louder, Joey. It's a good question.*

Joey: *It says you're going, you're riding at a constant speed up the hill. But the part that's going down, that point is, that's the top of the hill. How can you be above the top of the hill?*

Phil: *Come show us the points that you're talking about.*

(Joey comes up to the document camera.)

Joey: *Right here. If that's the top of the hill* (points at the lowest point of the graph), *how can he be up here?* (points at the flat portion of the graph, to the left of the lowest point on the graph) *Wouldn't he have to be right up here?* (points at a part of the graph that is higher than the flat portion of the graph)

Steven: *Because! Because that's the, the y-axis is the speed. Not the hill. It's the speed.*

Sarah: *You're riding at a constant speed. And then you hit a hill. Then you go up a hill.*

Steven: *Yeah. And you're going down the hill after.*

Sarah: *So, then you gradually accelerate.*

Steven: *Because you're going down. The speed gradually picks up.*

(After the class discussed Joey's question, Phil spoke with his students about the value of in-progress thinking.)

Phil: *How many people also wondered about Joey's question?*

(More than half of the students in the class raised their hands.)

Phil: *See, Joey, you're not alone.*

Joey: *Okay.*

Phil: *Almost everybody thought about it like that. Thanks for sharing that with us.*

After the lesson, Phil interpreted this classroom episode:

> Once I was able to get Joey to speak to the class, I stepped back to see how this would affect the understanding for other students. Some who thought they understood realized, through Joey's rough draft talk, that they were no longer sure if they understood. After, more students did get involved in the conversation, which squared away the understanding for the class. Afterward, I explicitly pointed out how Joey's rough draft talk allowed all of us to have a better understanding of speed versus time.
>
> —Phil Wandless

Phil amplified the strengths of Joey's contribution to the discussion by pointing out that Joey's question was useful for the group. Phil normalized that this was a question that most of the class shared. He observed that it was useful for the group to work on Joey's question together. Indeed, the class needed to take on Joey's question to keep learning. If we recognize that knowing and doing mathematics is a complex process that involves a range of strengths, then we can notice and amplify the many capabilities among our students.

Interactions between a teacher and students can challenge students' ideas of what it means to enact smartness in the mathematics classroom.

> "Students in our classroom recognize that every child has something intellectual to offer and something intellectual to learn. None of us knows everything, and we need each other to learn more." (Jilk 2016, 190)

Together, teachers and students could strive to interact in ways that reflect this norm.

Assigning competence is when teachers publicly name when a student enacts an intellectual strength that furthers the group's mathematical understandings (Jilk [2016] citing Cohen and Lotan [1997]). When teachers assign competence to students, they can shift students' ideas about what it means to be good at math and who can be good at it. If we invite rough draft thinking, we are likely to have more opportunities to disrupt students' assumptions about who is and is not good at math. We can point out many more ways of being smart in math, like posing a helpful question, and more students can see mathematical strengths in their peers and in themselves.

Our Orientations—as Teachers—for Promoting Rough Draft Thinking

A purpose of this book is to think together about how to create classrooms where rough draft thinking is invited. This means classrooms where students have opportunities to learn mathematics by having the freedom to say and write what makes sense to them so that they can be challenged to continue to grow in their thinking. We want students to feel safe sharing their dead ends.

After all, teaching is an act of empathy. As teachers, we relate to our students in terms of what it's like to make sense of something new. We try to make sense of our students' thinking about mathematics, just as our students try to make sense of mathematical ideas. All of us—teachers and students—are in a vulnerable position of learning something new, whether we are learning new mathematics or new ways of seeing and thinking about mathematics.

Compassionate, empathetic teaching involves embracing students' thinking where it is, today. Many of my undergraduates strive to teach empathetically. One teacher candidate, Selina, reflected, "I wanted to really listen to what the students explained, what the kids were saying, rather than what I wanted to hear." Take a look at Selina's recording of a second-grade student's thinking for the problem 27 + 15 in Figure 1.3.

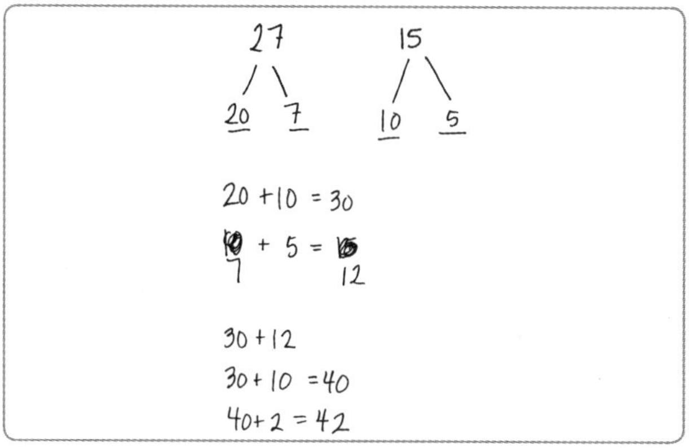

Figure 1.3
Selina's recording of Carlos's thinking

Her student, Carlos, decomposed 27 into 20 and 7 and 15 into 10 and 5. We can see some scribbles recorded by Selina around 7 and 12. Selina reflected on this experience:

> There was a moment in the second number problem when Carlos was explaining that he added the 7 + 5 to get 12. I had misunderstood him, and he began to get jumbled up, but I took a second to look at what I had written. I realized what he had said and fixed it on the board. I then reexplained what he had meant. I was proud that I did not get myself worked up over messing up, but really tried hard to understand what Carlos meant. This was one of those teacher moments that I will always remember.
>
> —Selina, preservice elementary mathematics teacher

Understanding how another person thinks is not easy. It may have been temporarily simpler for Selina to assume she knew what Carlos meant rather than admit that she misunderstood him initially. Empathetic teaching means we set aside our own discomforts, like Selina's feelings about "messing up." We direct our focus away from ourselves onto our students and challenge our assumptions about what we think we heard. Selina compassionately slowed down until she and Carlos seemed to understand each other.

Really hearing our students not only helps them learn but also makes them feel valued as people. Max Ray-Riek (2011) gave a powerful Ignite talk about *listening to* students rather than *listening for* what we want to hear from students. In his talk, he shared a memory from his experiences as a young child in school. The teacher asked him to share his thinking aloud:

> "The class listened to my idea. They realized that I had mathematical ideas in my head that no one else had ever thought about before. And that actually changed my life, being invited up to the room, to tell the class my ideas."

Listening to our students is not only productive for their learning but also powerful for developing their identities as learners. The distinction between listening to students rather than for an answer is useful for teachers to consider when promoting rough draft thinking.

Listening to Students' Thinking: Multiple Approaches

The research of Brent Davis (1997) helps us think about different ways of listening to students' thinking (Table 1.1) and their implications.

Are we engaging in evaluative listening (listening *for*) or more interpretive listening and hermeneutic listening (listening *to*)? Through interpretive listening, teachers try to understand the meanings that students are making of mathematics through asking questions. Hermeneutic listening is more interactive. Teachers and students build their understandings together through interacting. Both interpretive and hermeneutic listening align well with a practice of promoting rough draft thinking. During interpretive listening, students engage in sharing their rough draft thinking while teachers listen. During hermeneutic listening, both teachers and students engage in communicating their rough draft thinking together with one another, and the entire class's thinking develops, including the teacher's.

WAYS OF LISTENING TO STUDENTS' THINKING

Evaluative	Listening for what we expect to hear or want to hear. The goal in evaluative listening is to notice, find, and address errors or to notice, find, and point out correct thinking. Evaluative thinking is used to make judgments.
Interpretive	Making the effort to understand students' thinking. Teachers ask questions that elicit students to elaborate, so teachers can have access to more of students' ideas. The teacher acts as a listener and "the listener is aware of the fallibility of his or her sense-making" of the student's thinking (Davis 1997, 364). Yet, to some degree, the teacher remains an authority in the classroom about what counts as correct conceptions.
Hermeneutic	The teacher interacts with students in a way that the students develop new understandings and the teacher learns alongside students. The teacher shares authority with students when making sense of mathematics.

TABLE 1.1

> "Hermeneutic questions are ones to which the questioner does not know the answer (indeed, the answer may not yet exist), but there is a desire on the part of the questioner to know. The question is thus posed within a context in which he or she believes some contribution will be made toward its resolution." (Davis 1997, 360)

Teachers' curiosity matters when listening. During interpretive listening, a teacher could be genuinely curious about students' thinking. But a teacher is genuinely curious about both students' thinking and the mathematics when using hermeneutic questions. In contrast, evaluative listening limits teachers' opportunities to hear and appreciate students' rough draft thinking.

Moving Forward

Let's move forward together to learn alongside one another. As I collaborated with teachers to work on incorporating rough drafts in mathematics classrooms, the lens of rough draft math provided new insights on familiar problems for all of us. Whenever I interact with other teachers about rough draft thinking, they productively surprise me by how they use rough draft math to address a variety of dilemmas in their teaching practice. In the chapters of this book, we will think about these dilemmas and how rough draft math provided opportunities to work on them.

Chapter 2: Building a Culture of Rough Draft Thinking

One ongoing challenge we face in the mathematics classroom is creating an inclusive environment where all students feel safe to participate. If rough draft math occurs when we communicate to work on understanding, then we can create a safe space by normalizing that we are all constantly working to understand more. Setting a norm that we can all keep learning more from one another through sharing rough draft thinking leads to greater participation from more students and an exploratory atmosphere in the mathematics classroom. In Chapter 2, we will explore how rough drafts help us establish a classroom culture of sense-making, a culture of embracing opportunities to learn from one another's unfinished thinking, and a culture of continually pushing to learn more and more about mathematics together.

Chapter 3: Tasks That Provide Opportunities to Communicate to Learn

The tasks students encounter impact whether they can readily engage in rough draft thinking. In Chapter 3, we will think about selecting and enacting tasks to open up opportunities to develop new understandings that we can revisit and revise. Perhaps some of our students resist explaining why their solutions make sense if they know their answers are correct. Explaining could feel pointless to them. Purposefully selected and enacted mathematical tasks can help these students see reasoning as a goal and communication as a necessary part of doing mathematics. In Chapter 3, we will explore features of tasks that open pathways for communicating to learn.

Chapter 4: Refining Understanding Through Revising in Mathematics Class

Once we invite students to share unfinished, rough draft thinking through tasks that promote sense-making, a new challenge arises: How can we structure opportunities for students to refine their thinking? We do not want students' thinking to remain in a rough stage. In addition, how can we help students become metacognitively aware of their thinking, including how and why it has shifted? In Chapter 4, we will consider a range of instructional approaches that have the potential to explicitly promote revising in math classrooms.

Chapter 5: Rough Draft Thinking as a Rehumanizing Endeavor

Teachers' efforts to promote rough draft math have provided their students with positive experiences. Students felt more comfortable talking in front of the class and felt more valued as people. Previously, these students may have felt dehumanized in mathematics class or less comfortable and not as valued. In Chapter 5, we will explore how secondary teachers enacted instructional practices aligned with rough draft math that rehumanized mathematics learning experiences for students.

Chapter 6: Putting "It" into Practice . . . or We Are All Works in Progress

When I wrote Chapter 6, I took on the challenge of applying what I learned from writing this book. This chapter is my story about enacting rough draft math in my own teaching practice. I tried to illustrate that there is no one right way to enact rough draft math. The story also shows that we do not have to enact every element of rough draft thinking to enjoy a productive experience with our students. If we treat our own teaching practice as a work in progress, we'll persevere to keep improving.

We are all constantly learning—about mathematics, about teaching, and about the world—through sharing rough draft ideas. Along these lines, Fawn Nguyen (2016) wrote a blog post titled "7 Deadly Sins of Teaching [Maths]."

> Talking, talking, you're still talking. I pretty much end every workshop with this reminder: The more you talk, the less your kids learn. I plan each lesson using this as my go-to guiding principle. Math is a highly social endeavor, so for the love of Ramanujan and Lovelace, please stop talking so much so your kids may talk! Every question you pose is an opportunity for your kiddos to ponder (quietly by oneself first) and share their thoughts with peers. Every question! If you fret that your kids don't talk in class, then I wonder about two things: (1) Do students feel *safe* enough to talk in your class? and (2) Is the question you're asking interesting/worthwhile/challenging to even bother? (I must have asked hundreds of lame, boring, worthless questions but I'm not giving up. I practice and get better.)
>
> —Fawn Nguyen, middle school math teacher

I love what Fawn has to say here. Rough draft math is a way to invite more learners to communicate so they can be the ones engaging in making sense of mathematics. Inviting rough drafts helps students feel safe. But Fawn also reminds me that we need to give students something worth talking about together, which Chapter 3 will address directly. Most of all, I am inspired by Fawn's openness about how she is constantly revising and improving as a teacher. I relate. Rough drafts are for math, and they are for continually improving our teaching practice. I hope our journey together in this book inspires us all to not give up, to keep getting better at giving students opportunities to communicate to learn.

CHAPTER TWO

BUILDING A CULTURE OF ROUGH DRAFT THINKING

Learning is a process filled with twists and turns. To invite students to engage in rough draft mathematics, it helps to be explicit that a zigzagging process of thinking is normal as we develop new understandings. Students learn to anticipate and even appreciate bumpy moments of learning together. Through communicating, we start to make more sense of our thinking, and we can continue to grow our ideas by making them public.

How do we help students experience a spirit of rough drafting in a math class? In this chapter, we will explore how teachers set up their classroom cultures so students communicate to make sense of math together rather than perform. We talk to learn. The mathematics teachers in this chapter explicitly invite students to talk about their rough drafts and to revise their work. They talk with their students about the value of discussing their rough drafts, establishing explicit norms for interacting, assigning mathematical tasks that are worth talking about, and helping students learn to talk with one another by using sentence starters. First, let's visit a sixth-grade mathematics classroom.

Brandy's Dilemma: Needing to Move Away from Show-and-Tell

Brandy Cooper teaches mathematics to sixth-grade students in Milford, Delaware. I worked closely with Brandy during her eighth year of teaching. She has been honored for her work as a mathematics teacher; in 2016, she was selected as teacher of the year for her school district. Brandy constantly works to improve her teaching practice.

Brandy identified a dilemma that she wanted to address related to the culture of her classroom. She wanted to see and hear her students make more connections among their solutions. She wanted her students to build on one another's ideas to create larger understandings than they would have had prior to discussing their thinking. But, from Brandy's perspective, her whole-class discussions currently were more like a show-and-tell by the students and less like students learning from one another.

Brandy was aware of the five practices for orchestrating effective mathematics classroom discussions (Smith et al. 2009), so she would monitor students' group work, carefully select which students she would call on and in what order, and make the effort to work with students to bring forth connections. But she felt that the discussions still lacked a certain energy from the students. She observed that students did not seem to listen closely to one another, did not really use one another's thinking, and did not seem to express a sense of enthusiasm and interest in the ideas of their peers.

Brandy shared this dilemma with me when she participated in a study group that I led with secondary mathematics teachers in Delaware. In this study group, we read about and discussed Barnes's idea of exploratory talk (2008). During exploratory talk, students talk to work on developing their understanding. I was engaged in genuine inquiry with the teachers in this exploratory talk study group. We all wanted to understand how to foster exploratory talk in our mathematics classrooms. I thought that these teachers would be excited by the idea of incorporating exploratory or rough draft talk in math class, but I was uncertain about the range of ways that these teachers would want to enact rough draft thinking on a practical level. We codeveloped instructional strategies to work out those practicalities.

Each teacher in the study group identified a problem in their classroom that they wanted to address. Brandy thought that rough draft talk appeared to be a solution to her problem. Brandy unpacked her dilemma further. She said, "I have struggled in the past with finding a good stopping point partway through a problem for share-outs. It seemed that I would always let my students work too long and then have some students with completed work and others with nothing." She wondered whether it would make a difference to change when she stopped students from working in their small groups to present their thinking publicly to the class.

A "final draft," or "presentational talk," lens helped Brandy interpret what may have been happening during faltering share-outs. Maybe students were presenting final draft solutions. Students may have been in performance mode rather than in learning mode. For students to continue learning together while sharing out, Brandy decided she wanted to encourage exploratory, rough draft talk.

Brandy shifted her classroom culture by creating a round of rough draft sharing into her mathematics lessons, while her students worked on a challenging problem in their small groups. She would ask the groups to talk about their rough draft solutions with the class before they were completely finished working on the problem. To encourage students to present their rough drafts, Brandy explicitly discussed the value of learning from in-progress ideas. She clarified that the purpose of sharing drafts was to continue to learn from one another.

BRANDY'S NEW ROUTINE: A ROUND OF ROUGH DRAFT SHARING

- Launch problem.
- Students engage in initial rough draft thinking about strategies together in small groups.
- Students share out rough draft thinking to the large group. Peers may ask questions about their strategies or thinking or comment on what they notice. They do not make evaluative statements about correctness.
- Revise: second round of rough draft thinking in small groups.
- Second round of group presentations to large groups.
- Repeat as needed.

Brandy described the process in her own words:

When I first show them the problem, I ask them to engage in rough draft thinking. After a few minutes, they get up and share their rough draft thinking. Although it is sometimes incomplete, it often sparks ideas for other students who are listening to those presenting. I then ask my students to finish their rough draft thinking and move into final draft thinking. After having time with their small groups and listening to others' ideas during presentations, they are often ready to commit to a strategy and find a final answer. Students then present final draft thinking, which leads to whole-group discussion. I do this on a regular basis in my classroom, several times a week.

Generally, I put a problem up on the whiteboard. I tell my students they will have a few minutes to engage in rough draft talk in their small groups. After a few minutes, students bring their ideas up to the document viewer to present to the class. Sometimes, I ask specific groups to present or that they present in a certain order, and other times, I just let them volunteer in any order. It depends on what I hear them discussing as I circulate through the room.

During rough draft presentations, I do not allow my students to comment on whether or not they think the presenters are correct. They may only ask them questions about their strategies or their thinking.

After they have had a few minutes to listen, they go back to discussions with their groups. They are comparing their original ideas to presenters' ideas, and they have a much clearer understanding of whether they were originally on the right track or if they saw an idea that made them realize they were not. I usually hear some pretty good rough draft talk at this point because they have so many different ideas to consider and compare.

> [After a significant amount of additional work time has passed,] I then have students present their ideas for a second time. Generally, at this point, most groups have come to a correct solution, using multiple strategies. This time, students may comment on "correctness" in addition to asking questions about the groups' thinking and strategies.
>
> I think it's during presentations [when students present and discuss their rough drafts] that the best rough draft talk happens in my class. This is when they are questioning each other and thinking out loud, while others have the opportunity to jump in and share their thinking as well. If my students are still all over the place after two rounds of this, I usually ask them a question or point to a specific part of the problem to help guide their thinking before I let them go through another round. This structure has been working really well for the group of students I have this year.
>
> —Brandy Cooper, middle school math teacher

During rough draft sharing, Brandy asked students to focus on trying to understand one another's thinking rather than correct it. She encouraged her students to shift from evaluative listening to more interpretive, non-evaluative listening when peers shared their rough drafts. Shifting away from evaluative listening became a community effort that the teachers and students made together. It was not just the teacher's effort. This shift seemed to support students' ability to learn more from one another during discussions.

I wanted to know more, so I went to Brandy's classroom to observe her rough draft sharing routine in action. Brandy implemented the *Security Camera* task from the Mathematics Assessment Resource Service (2011) materials (Figure 2.1). (Before reading about Brandy's interactions with her students, try working on your own rough draft thinking about the problem so that you will be better able to consider these students' drafts of their thinking.)

A shop owner wants to prevent shoplifting.

He decides to install a security camera on the ceiling of his shop.

The camera can turn right round through 360°.

The shop owner places the camera at point P, in the corner of the shop.

The plan view shows where ten people are standing in the shop.

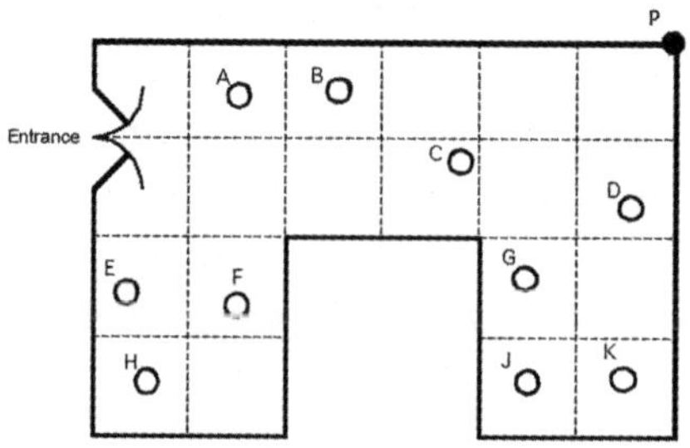

1. Which people cannot be seen by the camera at P? Explain your answer, showing clearly on the diagram how you know.

2. The shop owner says, "15% of the shop is hidden from the camera." Show clearly that he is correct.

Figure 2.1
Security Camera problem

Brandy's students sat in groups of four. Each student had access to a small dry erase board and markers. Students had role cards that described expectations for working together. To launch the task, Brandy displayed the image from the task for the class to see, and each student had their own copy of the worksheet.

> **Brandy:** *I'm not going to tell you anything about how we're going to solve this problem. I put up on the whiteboard the same thing that's on your paper. It's completely up to you how you want to do this today. I don't know that we'll finish it. It depends on how long it takes. We're just going to do one part to start. Who can tell me what 360 degrees means?*
>
> **Student:** *A full circle.*
>
> **Brandy:** *Every letter with a white circle is a person. Who cannot be seen with the camera? Convince us with some kind of math, some kind of model—how you know for sure. This is just rough draft time. But eventually we're going to prove it.*

Brandy took pressure off of students by telling them they were just going to get started today, and she let them know that they would have all of the time that they needed. She told them that "this is just rough draft time" so the students knew that initial ideas were valued, but they were not expected to figure the problem out on the first try.

While students were working in groups, Brandy circulated the room and monitored their work by looking at their whiteboards and listening to the group's conversations. To transition to whole-group sharing, she asked the students to wrap up some of their rough draft work in groups. "A couple more ideas for rough drafts and we're just going to share our initial thoughts."

Before she had students come up to share their thinking, Brandy reinforced the idea of nonevaluative listening to peers' thinking.

> **Brandy:** *We're not deciding if people are correct or incorrect. We're just listening to how they did it, why they did it. Who would like to go up first with rough draft talk?*

Students eagerly raised their hands. It appeared as if many students wanted to share. This round of rough draft sharing seemed like something students were used to doing. Brandy let a student decide who talked first.

> **Brandy:** *Nick, you may choose the first group. Whether you're done or not done, listen to what this group has to say. We're not deciding if they're right or wrong. We're just listening to their ideas. First of all, which letters can we not see?*

Two students went up to the document camera. Brandy also had a wireless microphone that students held to amplify their voices, and the students seemed comfortable using it.

> **Kevin:** *F and H, there's this wall here, if you were imagining this in real life, there was this blocking of a wall here, you probably wouldn't be able to see it, there would be the wall blocking them.*
>
> **Malik:** *This is how you can prove it.*
>
> **Kevin:** *Exactly, that's what I did.*

Malik (draws the line shown in Figure 2.2)**:** *You can't see H. You can't see F. Look at that.*

Brandy: *Does anybody have a question for them?*

Helena: *How would you figure out that, if you know it wasn't glass? How did you know it's not glass walls?*

Kevin: *I'm just making an inference. I'm not trying to be smart, but if it was a glass wall, they would have asked a different question.*

(Brandy clarified that it was not a glass wall.)

Brandy: *Any other questions? You can choose another group to share.*

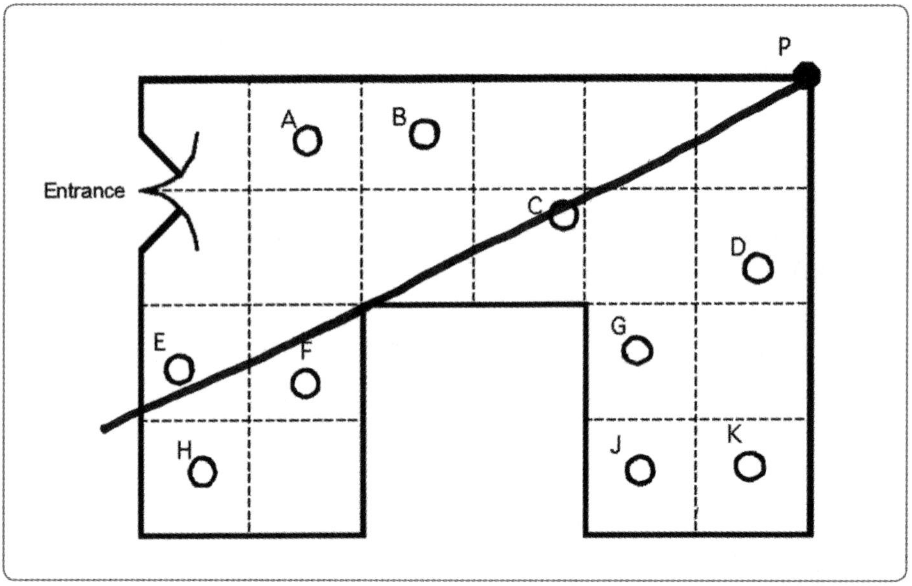

Figure 2.2
Malik's security camera sight line

When I observed Brandy's students sharing ideas, I noticed that students genuinely tried to come up with questions that were targeted to the thinking of their peers. This was evidence to me that the students were attempting to listen to one another, because the teacher expected that they would comment on and even wonder about their peers' thinking.

The question about whether the walls could have been glass reminded me of a problem-posing technique—wondering what-if-not? Stephen Brown and Marion Walter (1983) describe this useful approach to mathematics problem posing in their classic book, *The Art of Problem Posing*. What if the constraints change? What can we learn about the problem in its current set of constraints if we change them? In this case, what if the walls were see-through? Then what could be seen or not seen? Wait, how do we know, or how did they know that the walls were not glass? The student posed a question to see whether it would help the group and the class make sense of a situation. As students try to understand their peers' thinking, they could develop new curiosities and wonderments about their peers' work or about the problem itself.

The class worked together to negotiate meaning about the diagram by wondering together and talking about false starts and stops.

Melissa: *I took the ruler and drew a second line* (Figure 2.3). *Now the camera could see E.*

Maya: *Melissa, I have a question, Why does your other line go through the wall?*

Melissa: *I was trying to see if my line could go to F, but it just went through the wall.*

Jason: *I disagree, you can see F and H, it's a glass wall.*

Brandy: *We're not conspiracy theorists here. When I walked around the first time, you* (Melissa) *thought it was E, F, and H. But then you thought the only one they couldn't see was H.*

Melissa: *They could see the letters, not the people* (circles). *They can't see the actual people. At first, I thought the letters were the people.*

Maya: *Then why would they put the circles there?*

Brandy: *Good point. Let's have one last person share.*

Chuck: *F and H can't be seen. E, he thought he was sneaky, but the camera can see E. F and H are behind the wall somewhere.*

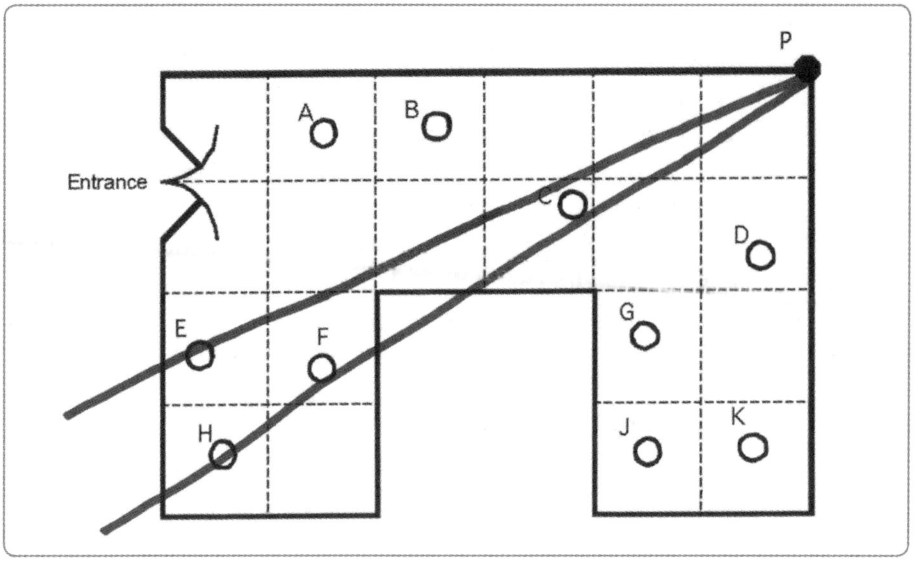

Figure 2.3
Melissa's security camera sight lines

During rough draft sharing, Brandy asked students to talk about changes to their thinking. For example, she pointed out that the students who initially thought only one person would not be seen by the camera shifted after spending additional time on the problem and hearing peers' perspectives. Asking students to share their revisions is an important part of exploring rough drafts in math class. Students can become aware of growth and shifts in their ideas. Other students can feel validated if they originally thought similarly. They have a chance to articulate why their ideas do and do not make sense, which supports their learning. Sharing revisions normalizes that our mathematical thinking constantly evolves and that we are not expected to land on the best way to think about a problem on the first attempt.

As a part of making sense of the diagram and being playful, the students wanted to talk more about the diagram during rough draft sharing.

> **Brandy:** *Now we all agree that F and H can't be seen, and it's not a glass wall?*
>
> **Nick:** *Why doesn't he install cameras in every corner?*

Helena: *Also, he could have mirrors.*

Brandy: *Hold on to those thoughts.*

Maya: *See how in the entrance, the door curves? A person could be right there.*

Brandy: *It's just a floor plan.*

Maya: *Maybe one of those spinny doors.*

One of the simultaneously beautiful and challenging aspects of opening up classroom talk is that sometimes students will discuss the problem in ways that surprise us. Maybe their ideas do not seem to relate to the problem. But if we don't ask the students what they think, they might continue to think about the problem's context in ways that prevent them from making sense of the mathematical relationships. As we listen to students, we will usually find that their thinking is connected to the task more than we might initially realize. We can encourage students to be themselves while talking about math, and we can enjoy their ideas and personalities. Brandy's openness to rough draft sharing allowed for briefly exploring the contextual situation so that students could next focus on the mathematical relationships under consideration.

Brandy: *Let's go back to rough draft math. James thinks 15 percent of the shop is hidden. How can you prove that? This is rough draft. How are you going to prove that 15 percent of the shop is hidden? Let's first listen to James as he shares his rough draft ideas.*

James: *The blocks are hidden, it will be 3 blocks. Three divided by 20 . . . times 5 . . . 15 divided by 100.*

Brandy: *In order to be 15 percent, it would have to be 3 out of 20? Is that right? Does anyone have a question for James of how he did it?*

There seemed to be multiple aspects to wonder about here. How did James decide that the hidden area was equivalent to three square units?

How did James determine that these square units represented 15 percent of the shop's area? Even when students are asked to wonder about one another's thinking, however, sometimes they do not ask one another questions during nonevaluative sharing. Instead, Melissa volunteered to restate James's thinking.

> **Melissa:** *Because a percent has to be out of 100. Five times what equals 100, so that's 20. Then so they can see the E in this square, took off this part, so 15 percent that you can't see.*

By gesturing while at the document camera (Figure 2.4), Melissa pointed to the diagram to show that a part of square E, the part that could not be seen, could fit into a part of square F that could be seen. The part of E that filled in the rest of F illustrated now that the equivalent of three square units were hidden from the camera.

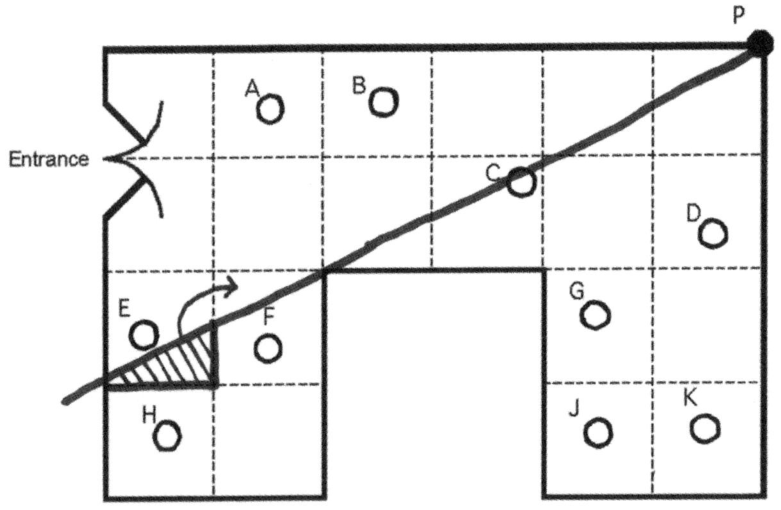

Figure 2.4
Melissa's observation

The area of the shop, 20 square units, represented 100 percent of the area. Melissa was trying to say that because the scale factor of 5 takes 20 square units to 100 percent of the area, then 3 square units that could not be seen, with a scale factor of 5, would be 15 percent of the area of the shop not being seen.

Restating one another's thinking is another form of nonevaluative engagement with a peer's ideas. It's as if Melissa was saying, this is what I heard you say, James, which is validating to James, because he feels heard. It's good for Melissa, because it helps her continue to make sense of James's thinking. It's also good for the classroom community, because it slows down the discussion so that the group can take time to hear the ideas more than once. For all these reasons, having students restate one another's thinking is a talk move that engages students in richer classroom discussions (Chapin, O'Connor, and Anderson 2003).

I appreciated the chance to see how Brandy promoted nonevaluative listening during rough draft sharing among her class so that students thought about one another's thinking. One shift that seems important is that, once Brandy changed the purpose of discussion from sharing final answers to sharing unfinished thinking—to understand one another's thinking in progress—students started to comment on and listen to one another, not only because their teacher communicated these expectations but also because the students were not fully finished with their solutions. Because their work was still in progress, they had more questions about one another's work than they would have had otherwise. They learned through talking. (For more on this idea of stopping groups early in their process and sharing out their emerging ideas in high school mathematics classrooms, see Webel [2010] about shifting authority from the teacher to the students.)

Brandy reflected on her new routine—the Round of Rough Draft Sharing—and why she enjoyed this approach that she developed.

> Before I started using the exploratory talk language in my classroom, I struggled with finding a natural stopping point early into a problem for ideas to be shared. I always seemed to let things go too long, and then my students were in presentational talk about their final answers during share-outs. I have gotten better at stopping by using the terms *rough draft thinking* and *final draft thinking*, since I have my students share out each type after some collaborative small-group work time.

> Before I started using this language, I found myself struggling with knowing when a good midpoint for sharing would be. For example, I would either let my groups go for too long, and then many would have a final answer, or I would cut them off too soon, and they were sharing ideas so incomplete that they weren't helpful to others. When I started using this language, I saw a difference in how my students engaged in collaborative learning.
>
> —Brandy Cooper

For Brandy, incorporating a round of rough draft sharing was a key instructional move to shift her classroom culture during whole-class discussions. She wanted the discussions to be when learning happened. She promoted the value of learning from one another and normalized that initial attempts will need revision.

Constructivism and Conceptual Understanding as the Foundation for Rough Draft Math

A principle underlying the use of rough draft math is that a significant goal of learning in mathematics classrooms is to develop conceptual understanding. Our current mathematics standards movement, the Common Core State Standards for Mathematics, adopted by most states in the United States, is designed in part to foster classrooms that give students opportunities to "pursue conceptual understanding, procedural skills and fluency, and application with equal intensity" (National Governors Association 2010). Conceptual understanding is comprehension of mathematical concepts, operations, and relationships among them (Kilpatrick, Swafford, and Findell 2001), characterized by connections between mathematical procedures and the ideas that underlie them (Hiebert and Carpenter 1992). Conceptual understanding does not mean that students do not learn mathematical procedures but that they develop procedural skills: (1) by developing an understanding of meanings underlying numbers and operations, and (2) by developing an understanding of the relationships underlying the procedures. There is power in developing understandings before teaching procedures (Leinwand et al. 2014).

If the goal in learning is to develop conceptual understanding, then the process of learning that underpins rough draft math is constructivism. Students learn from opportunities to engage in productive struggle and make sense of mathematics. From the perspective of constructivism (e.g., von Glasersfeld and Steffe 1991), learning is when students' prior knowledge is perturbed in some way, and through wrestling with trying to make sense of this cognitive dissonance, students accommodate their current understandings to include the new ideas. They rearrange what they already know to create relationships in their knowledge to allow the new idea to fit and make sense to them. Through engaging in reflective abstraction, new understandings are developed and solidified. Active learning, then, is when students are "attempting to interrelate, to reinterpret, [and] to understand new experiences and ideas" (Barnes 2008, 2).

Communication and social interaction aid the learning process from a constructivist perspective. Through talking and writing, students can make their current ways of thinking available to be reflected on and contrasted with others' ways of thinking. When students' current ways of thinking are contrasted with others' and they recognize a lack of fit or a disconnect in some way, students' thinking can be productively perturbed. Further dialogue, whether inner dialogue, conversation with another person, writing for oneself, or writing to an audience or another person, can support making sense of the potential ways that their dissonance can be resolved. Continuing to dialogue to reflect on this resolution leads to deeper understandings and new connections. Therefore, communication is a tool for learning throughout the process of constructing conceptual understanding.

Engaging students in rough draft math, then, aids the learning process as students expose current ways of thinking, the causes of their dissonance, and their rationales for revision. Brandy explains:

> To me, rough draft talk is a very low-pressure form of discourse for students. When I ask my students to engage in rough draft talk, it is at the beginning of a collaborative learning situation. A problem is presented to students, and my students' initial thought process is what I consider rough draft thinking. Sometimes, rough draft talk occurs solely within their small groups; sometimes, it is presented to the class as a rough draft. Even when it is presented, it is simply the sharing of initial thoughts and ideas. This is when the learning is still occurring. This varies greatly from presentational talk. When

> students engage in presentational talk, they have already worked through their initial ideas and come to a consensus on the correct path or strategy to solve the problem. When presentational talk is shared with the whole class, it is a final draft of a strategy with an answer. This is when the learning has come to a conclusion.
>
> —Brandy Cooper

I love how Brandy stated, "This is when the learning is still occurring." The beauty of opening up the classroom to rough draft thinking is that we see one another's learning taking place.

When students share their rough drafts, they can then compare and contrast these drafts with others', which requires both listening to peers and thinking about how peers' thinking relates to our own. If a peer's thinking seems similar to our own thinking, we are likely to assimilate our peer's ideas ("This is like my idea because . . ."). Seeing similarity is one way to make a connection that extends and deepens current ways of thinking. Alternatively, if we notice a difference between our way of thinking and a peer's way of thinking, we have an opportunity to determine whether this difference matters and whether we need to revise our thinking. Rough draft mathematics invites the active process of sense-making out of a student's inner dialogue and into collective space—either through talking with their teacher and peers or through writing that their teacher and, possibly, peers would read.

The opportunity to engage in rough draft math is shaped by which mathematics task we choose and how we implement this task. Whether students have a rich dialogue around mathematics—whether inner or outer dialogue—depends on what they are asked to do and think about. Not all mathematical tasks are rich enough to give students much to dialogue about and reflect on. In Chapter 3, we will delve into how mathematics problems we choose support learning through rough draft thinking.

Brandy's navigation of her dilemma illustrates how she used rough draft thinking to create a culture of learning in her classroom. She stopped small-group work before students had completely finished and had them share out in-progress thinking. She explicitly tagged their talk as *rough draft sharing*. Students were encouraged to take an interpretive, nonevaluative stance to their peers' thinking. They then had a chance to go back and revise their thinking further. But how can we begin to help students understand the purpose of rough drafts in mathematics class? Another Delaware teacher shared her approach with me.

Talking About Rough Draft Talk: Christine's Classroom

Christine Hubbard teaches seventh-grade at Meredith Middle School in Middletown, Delaware. She starts her school year by talking with her students about the role of rough drafts in learning. Then, she gives the students an opportunity to interact about their draft ideas during Number Talk. This Number Talk focuses on a Dot Pattern; students talk about different ways of seeing the total number of dots in a diagram. She sets up this Number Talk by talking about the purpose of rough drafts in mathematics class with her students. Below we can read about how this unfolded in her classroom.

> **Christine:** *Before we even start, I want to talk with you about this idea of* rough draft talk *versus* presentational talk. *Before I even say anything, think about language arts class or social studies. Maybe you've done a rough draft, and then you've done a presentation. Maybe your presentation was an essay. Maybe your presentation was speaking in front of the class about something. What is the difference? Think in your mind on your own for a moment about what the difference is between rough draft and a presentation.*
>
> (She waits.)
>
> **Christine:** *Now, what I want you to do is turn and talk to the person next to you. The person with the shortest hair, you're going to go first. Talk and tell what was in your mind about the difference between a rough draft and a final presentation. When you're done, give the other person a chance to talk as well. Okay?*
>
> (Students converse.)

She then had a discussion with her students about what they thought about rough drafts.

> **Christine:** *What's the difference between a rough draft in ELA* (English Language Arts) *and a final copy?*
>
> **Jacob:** *A rough draft is more unorganized, and then you're adding things and fixing things that were wrong. A final copy is neat, and it's organized, and it's done.*
>
> **Christine:** *So is a rough draft okay? Is it all right to do a rough draft? Are you supposed to do a rough draft? Yeah. Your teachers encourage you. Get those ideas out on paper. It should be the same when we're in math class, whether we're writing them down or whether we're just saying them. If you've got an idea about something and you're participating, your idea does not have to be perfect. Your idea can just be, like, rough draft.*

Christine wanted to let her students know explicitly what she thought about rough drafts after collecting her students' ideas.

> **Christine:** *These are some things to think about. Rough draft talk versus presentational talk, these are some extra things to think about. Rough draft talk sounds choppy. You hesitate when you're talking. Kind of repeating a little bit. You often need to take your time or restart your explanation. The beginning of an idea is there but needs to be further developed. And you're still thinking through your idea as you talk. This is a safe place for you to do that and to engage in rough draft talk.*
>
> *Presentational talk sounds smooth. It's well practiced. Ideas are fully formed, and appropriate vocabulary is used in your explanation. You're sharing an idea with others that has already been refined.*
>
> *Think about these two things. When we are in rough draft talk, that's when your learning is actually happening. It's happening in the moment. That's what we want, so we're excited when you're in rough draft talk. Please know, it's okay to do so. Okay, ready for your first Number Talk?*

As a part of norm setting before she had students engage in open strategy sharing early in the school year, Christine used the idea of rough draft talk to help her students to feel free to share ideas that were not fully formed, not refined. We want to help students understand that communicating can be used to make sense out of ideas, not just presenting what you already know.

Moving forward, we can invite students to tag and identify when they are sharing rough drafts. We'll hear students saying, "This is just my rough draft, but . . ." It is a nice move that they can use if they want to make it clear that their ideas are just now emerging. Students find this move freeing. When we teach, we can, as Brandy did, tag moments as opportunities to share rough draft ideas. Invite students to share by saying, "Let's hear your rough draft ideas." Students who might otherwise be unwilling to share their thinking will offer input during discussion if they are told that they are only expected to share a rough draft thought.

I've had discussions with teachers about whether they want to name this sort of talk as rough draft sharing or exploratory talk. Michael Reitemeyer, who worked at that time as a secondary mathematics coach in the Appoquinimink School District in Middletown, Delaware, after teaching high school in Wilmington, Delaware, prefers Barnes's original label—*exploratory talk*. He finds that emphasizing the activity of exploring and wondering about mathematics is useful for promoting students' agency. Other teachers prefer using *rough draft talk* rather than *exploratory talk*. Brandy explains her rationale.

> My students are familiar with the term *rough draft* from their English language arts classes, so it was an easy transition to make to math. When I use the term *rough draft* talk, it feels like it takes a lot of pressure off of the students. When just starting on a new problem, I want them to feel comfortable enough to take risks and share ideas. Before I started using this language, I would often just tell them to go ahead and begin work. I think it felt more formal, like they felt I was expecting them to get the correct answer right away. By using this language, it makes my classroom feel more relaxed during the learning, where there is no pressure to come up with the correct strategy or answer right away. However, I actually believe their learning progresses faster in a lot of cases, because they are feeling more comfortable in their conversations and their learning.
>
> —Brandy Cooper

Whether you and your students call this talk about emerging ideas *exploratory* or rough *rough draft talk*, what seems most important is removing the pressure to finding a "correct" way of thinking immediately. Instead, we invite students to continue to extend and refine their thinking. Michael Reitemeyer expressed to me that talk is valuable for the process of learning, because he sees it as the most flexible form of communication.

> Talk is so important during the exploratory, rough draft stage. Ideas are being formed and are still in their most malleable state. This is the time when meaning is most importantly negotiated, and talk is the medium where negotiation of meaning is taking place. Having students share these negotiations and notice that these negotiations took place is a really important metacognitive skill, in my opinion.
>
> —Michael Reitemeyer, supervisor of mathematics

It is helpful, then, for students to engage in rough draft talk soon after defining it with them. By trying out rough draft talk, they learn to believe in its usefulness through reflecting on their experience. After talking with her students about rough draft thinking, Christine engaged her students in a Number Talk about ways to visualize chunking a set of dots to make the set easier to count.

Christine: *I want you in your mind to be thinking about how many dots there are.*

Caleb: *It's like dominoes.*

Christine: *Yeah, you're going to see that some patterns might remind you of dominoes. I'm going to flash it up there. Try and see how you can figure out how many are up there without counting one by one.*

Christine also introduced hand signals for Number Talks, specifically putting a number of fingers at your chest to indicate how many strategies you have. A student asked, "A strategy is a different way of counting?" Christine said, "Exactly." After flashing up the image of the dots (Figure 2.5), Christine then collected answers—how many dots students saw. They all reported seeing eight dots.

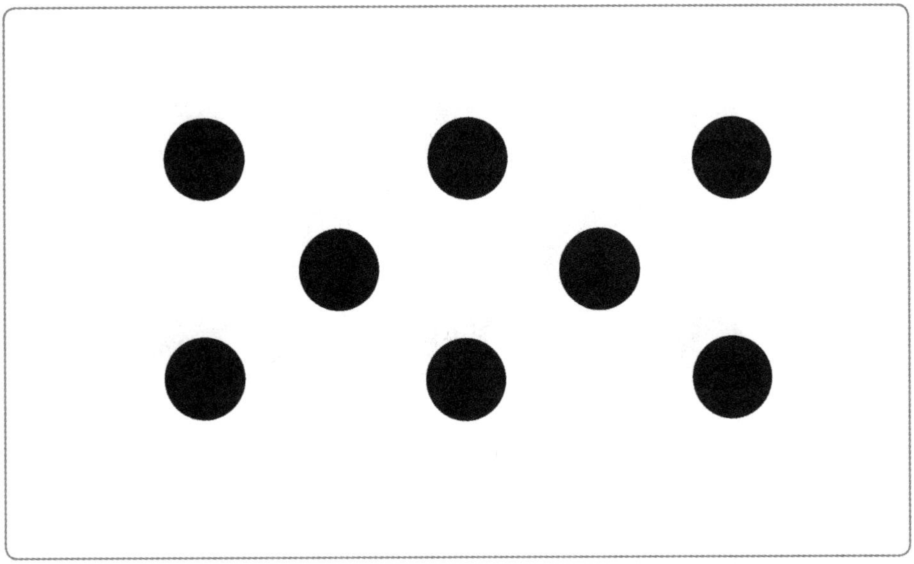

Figure 2.5
Dot Pattern for Christine's Number Talk

Christine then invited students to share: "Can anybody be brave enough to share and justify why they think there's eight dots up there?" A number of students went up to the whiteboard to draw how they grouped and chunked the diagram to count. The first student saw a set of five, as if it was a side of dice, plus three more. The second student saw the three on top, the three on the bottom, and the two in the middle. Another student came up to the front of the room and gestured to indicate diagonal lines:

> **Jason:** *So I saw these three and then these three. So there were six and then I made them into one sideways diamond. Then I added the two on the ends. To me this looks like a diamond.*
>
> **Christine:** *Jason's saying he sees a shape, is this what you're showing? What shape is that?* (Christine drew in lines as seen in Figure 2.6.)

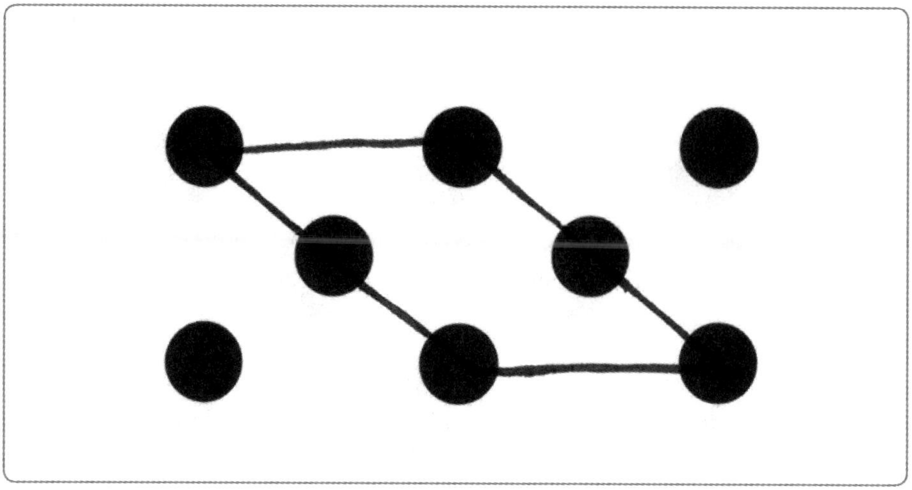

Figure 2.6
Jason sees a shape

Students brainstormed names for the shape, saying things like *pentagon*, *parallelogram*, *rhombus*, or "I can't remember." Christine identified the terms that students used and asked them to describe what they are (e.g., "What's a pentagon?"). Then she asked, "So what can we call that shape?" Jason replied, "A weird rectangle thing." Calista said, "It's a parallelogram." Another student shouted out, "It's a thingy!" Christine said, "Calista is telling us that it's a parallelogram." Then she went on to say, "Yeah, we could describe it either way, but if we call it a parallelogram, that's using more precise language that we can all visualize." Michael Reitemeyer, the math coach in Christine's district, was also in the room and asked, "So is it okay during rough draft talk to maybe call it a weird rectangle?" Christine turned to her students and said, "What do we think, as a class?" Students said, yes, so she said "Sure, we can accept it. Absolutely. Rough draft talk helps us."

There were multiple moments when students engaged in rough draft sharing during this Number Talk. The first was the moment the teacher intended, which was when students shared multiple ways of seeing how to chunk the diagram to count the total. This sort of exploratory talk invites multiple ways of seeing mathematical relationships. But there was a moment that Christine did not necessarily anticipate, which was rough draft talk around how Jason named the shape he saw in the diagram. She shifted back and forth with students from rough draft to more formal language to begin refining their rough draft talk, but then affirmed that the rough draft language of "a weird rectangle" was a useful way to get started talking about the shape. Taking moments to talk about talking is important, but it is even more important to give students firsthand experience engaging in rough draft talk and to name and label those rough draft moments.

Rights of the Learner and Labeling Work: Establishing Expectations for Working Together

Another way to let students know that their in-progress ideas are welcome is by promoting the Rights of the Learner. I learned about Rights of the Learner through Crystal Kalinec-Craig (2017a) at the University of Texas at San Antonio, who, in turn, learned about them through working with Olga Torres, a classroom teacher in Tucson, Arizona. If students' rights are named and validated, then they are more likely to feel entitled to talk about their rough draft ideas and, in turn, learn more from one another.

Here are some rights that learners could have in a mathematics classroom, although this list is not exhaustive:

RIGHTS OF THE LEARNER

Some possible examples:

1. The right to be confused.
2. The right to make mistakes.
3. The right to only say (or write) what makes sense TO YOU.
4. The right to revise your thinking.
5. The right to not be *defined* by what you say at one point in time.

These rights normalize experiences that learners have in mathematics classrooms: feeling unsure and being imperfect, using somewhat informal language, not using English all of the time, or changing your mind. These experiences are expected. They are students' rights. Students can say, "I'm using my right to revise my thinking right now," and they can share how their thinking evolved. If they make an error, they can say, "It's all right, it's my right to make a mistake." These rights can open up space for more students to feel competent as their thinking continues to grow and change during classroom discussions.

One approach to promoting rights is to create posters with learners' rights on them and introduce the posters by explaining to students that they have these rights. While doing so, we can explain to students why these rights matter. Suzi Sappington, a teacher at Appoquinimink High school in Middletown, Delaware, introduced her students to their rights and hung up posters of rights in her room. She then contacted me and said, "I wanted to let you know that after I showed these to my students last Wednesday, I feel like it set a great tone! One student actually said (with sincerity), 'I really like the vibe in here!' I told the students that I wanted them to voice their opinions about a right they feel wasn't represented." She invited her students to create their own rights.

Some teachers have introduced rights to students, as examples, and then give their students the power to draft a set of Rights of the Learner for their class. Michael Sanchez, a ninth-grade teacher at MOT Charter School in Middletown, Delaware, started his school year by asking students to brainstorm their rights in his classroom. His first period class came up with this list:

1. Right to make a mistake
2. Right to ask questions
3. Right to be confused
4. Right to be respected
5. Right to be silent
6. Right to not be judged
7. Right to ask for help
8. Right to pace yourself

9. Right not to know the answer
10. Right to feel safe
11. Right to be afraid

I love the idea of the right to be silent. We all need thinking time when we take a break from talking to actively listen or cognitively process an idea. The right to pace yourself is also brilliant because understanding occurs on its own timeline. It's hard to predict when things will make sense to you or when you will have a creative insight. The right to be afraid seems important as well, because even though we know that we have the right to be confused, to make mistakes, and to be unsure, it's okay that we feel afraid about those feelings at times. We recognize that some fear might be part of the process. It's okay to feel however we feel. When students create their rights, they not only have ownership of them but you will also have a better sense of what forms of support they need.

The rights do not need to be static. The class can revisit and revise rights periodically. If students rewrite and draft new rights for their classroom, their rights as learners become a living set of ideas.

In addition, if students are encouraged to name and claim when their rights are being met, they benefit from recognizing their rights in practice. Students might say, "I'm using my right to say this in a way that makes sense to me," when explaining their thinking. Alternatively, we could point out when students are enacting their rights, "I noticed that you enacted your right to ask a question." It helps to reinforce these rights through asking students to reflect on them and pointing out when students enact them.

Along with posting rights, teachers can create posters of expectations for classroom interactions to display and discuss when developing a classroom culture of sense-making in mathematics. One of my favorite sets of expectations is from Sara VanDerWerf (2016b) for Number Talks at the secondary level. I find these expectations useful for talking about mathematics generally.

Regarding the first expectation, one thing I love is that it promotes the notion that doing mathematics is not only about solving but about seeing in many ways. In the second expectation, all students are encouraged to see how their ideas matter for the learning of the classroom community. The third expectation amplifies the role of listening and recognizes that it is an important form of active participation.

SARA VANDERWERF'S EXPECTATIONS FOR WORKING TOGETHER DURING NUMBER TALKS

1. There are many ways to see or do any problem.
2. Everyone is responsible for communicating his or her thinking clearly to help others' understanding.
3. Everyone is responsible for trying to understand each other's thinking.

When Allison Hintz (2011) interviewed fourth graders about their participation, she learned that listening actively during a mathematics classroom discussion offered students benefits, such as growing their repertoire of strategies over time, checking their answer or their thinking, and learning more efficient ways or a way that might make even more sense. I honor the powerful role of listening during class discussions because of the intellectual demands involved with making sense of another person's thinking. Also, listening to someone and working hard to understand is a way of respecting and demonstrating that you care about them. Therefore, active listening is an essential component of classroom norms.

Students gradually become accustomed to sharing their thinking while it is still in progress, but it can involve an adjustment period. When a colleague of mine, Eva Thanheiser at Portland State University, taught a mathematics content course for future elementary teachers and asked students to share their rough draft thinking, initially the future teachers said things like, "She asked us to share our work, and we weren't even done yet." It was frustrating to the students to share unfinished work. We collaborated to develop an intervention for her students (Figure 2.7).

Barely Started	Partway Done	Almost Done	Totally Done
We have *no idea* whether we are correct.	We *might be* correct.	We are *pretty sure* that we are correct.	We are *very certain* that we are correct.

Figure 2.7
Labels for unfinished work (Thanheiser and Jansen 2016, 146)

In Eva's class, students worked in groups on challenging mathematics tasks and created posters that represented their work. For the intervention, we asked students to label their group's product as to how complete or correct they thought it was. They put this label on their posters before they hung them on the wall. We thought that the label would allow for face-saving because the students would be the ones to point out that they were or were not finished. The students would be able to clarify how confident they were about their work. We hoped that, by asking the future teachers to label their work before sharing, we would communicate that it's okay to share work in progress during this class. By the end of the semester, this labeling process helped the future teachers become more aware of the value of sharing their work at any stage.

Siobahn Tried Brandy's Approach: A New Dilemma

Siobahn Suppa and I both have taught future elementary teachers. One semester, she was teaching a course at the University of Delaware in which preservice teachers have opportunities to develop their mathematics content knowledge for teaching. Specifically, the future teachers have opportunities to expand their mathematical knowledge by developing a deeper understanding for meanings underlying mathematical concepts and operations—or why procedures work.

Siobahn had talked with me about rough draft thinking before, heard me speak about it, and read about it (Jansen et al. 2017). She felt ready to try engaging her learners in rough draft thinking, and she thought that a good way to do this would be to implement Brandy's approach of a Round of Rough Draft Sharing. So, she launched a task, invited her students to work in groups, and then stopped the groups before they were done to have them share their thinking in progress. She told her class that this was *rough draft sharing*, and they were expected to ask questions after their colleagues presented their current thinking.

A new dilemma arose. Very few students asked one another questions. The magic did not happen for her and her students. This was interesting to me. I asked Siobhan to tell me more.

She was working with future elementary teachers on thinking about meanings of rational numbers, specifically the meaning of the denominator as *the size of the piece*, when the unit is equally partitioned that number of times, and the meaning of the numerator as *the number of pieces*. For instance, three-fourths is three pieces of size one-fourth. The pieces of size one-fourth are made by equally partitioning a unit four times.

The future teachers were working on the tasks in Figure 2.8. (This task was written by Eric Sisofo, one of my University of Delaware colleagues.)

Fractions as Measurements on a Number Line

Directions: Indicate where each of the following numbers is located on the number lines below. **Be as precise as you can.**

#	Picture for Fractional Amount
$\frac{3}{4}$	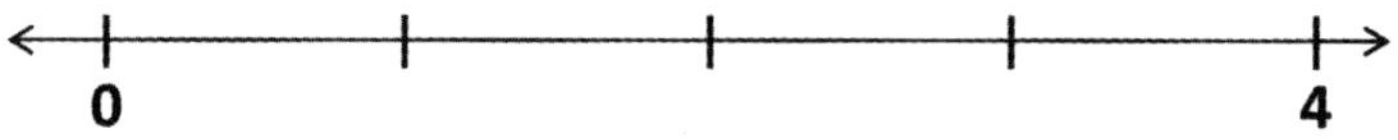
$2\frac{1}{3}$	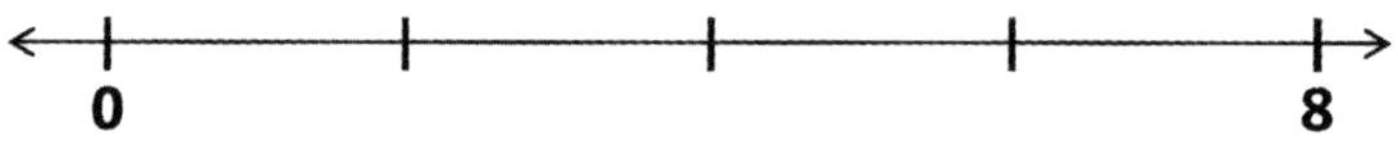
$1\frac{5}{12}$	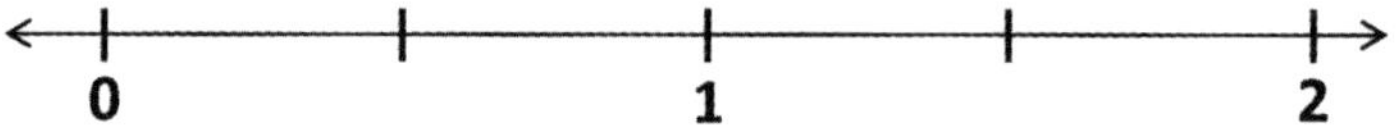
$\frac{17}{6}$	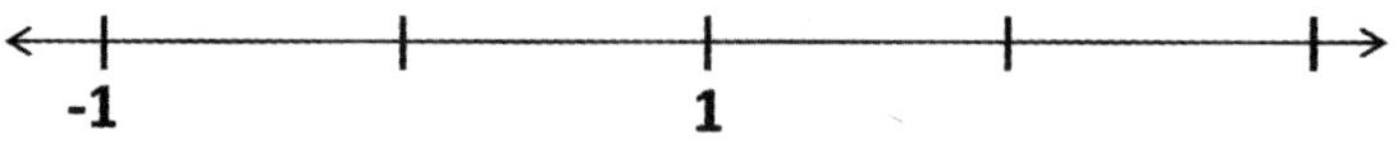

Figure 2.8
Task from Siobahn's class

In a previous class, the preservice teachers had created fraction strips by folding unit strips into different increments. The process of folding each strip into halves, thirds, fourths, and so on was intended to help preservice teachers experience that, as the denominator number increases, the size of the piece decreases. Siobahn wanted the preservice teachers to discuss their process of placing the rational number on the number line by determining what counted as a unit of one on the number line, equally partitioning each unit the number of times indicated by the denominator, and then counting out the number of pieces in the numerator.

Siobahn attempted to cut off small groups before they were finished. She wanted to open the floor to the preservice teachers, anticipating they would discuss placing 1 and $\frac{5}{12}$ on the number line. She hoped that they would talk about $\frac{17}{12}$ as equivalent to 1 and $\frac{5}{12}$, about equally partitioning the unit for denominator, and about counting out the number of pieces for the numerator.

Interrupting the preservice teachers before they were finished made Siobahn feel uncomfortable, but she tried it anyhow. She asked one student, Penelope, to share her thinking, and then Siobahn asked the class, "Does anyone have any thoughts about that?" Penelope's model was accurate, but Siobahn thought that the preservice teachers could still comment on her thinking. No one responded to Siobahn's question. Siobahn asked again, "Does anyone have anything to share about what they notice?" Again, more silence. Siobahn then asked an alternative question, considering that her audience was prospective teachers, "What do you think a student might ask Penelope if she was teaching right now?" Her class still did not respond.

Siobahn then decided to model for her students how to talk about Penelope's thinking. She said, "Okay, I have one: *How did you put twelfths on the number line?*" Then the class started talking! They discussed different ways they partitioned one unit into twelfths, such as first in fourths and then in thirds, first in thirds and then in fourths, or first sixths by making thirds of halves and then twelfths by making halves of sixths. Sharing their strategies was something that the preservice teachers understood how to talk about. They knew there were multiple ways of working on something mathematically. To get at her goal for students' thinking, even though it didn't come up organically, Siobahn then said, "Notice that in Penelope's model, she partitioned a unit into twelfths. Shaded one of them. That one piece, one-twelfth, can be a quantity on its own. Then we can count out copies of twelfths."

This class discussion did not sit well with Siobahn. She tried to initiate rough draft thinking by stopping the groups before they were done to have a round of rough draft sharing, but the students did not have much to say. The talk did not feel exploratory.

Together, we made some conjectures as to why the students didn't interact much during this point in the class. Siobahn conjectured:

1. I didn't interrupt them quickly enough. The students were actually done rather than still in progress.
2. The task wasn't at the appropriate level. Maybe it wasn't challenging enough. They didn't have any questions. Not problematic enough to have something to discuss.
3. I didn't have the goals explicit enough to help me guide where I want the discussion to go.

I offered additional conjectures:

4. They didn't understand the purpose of rough draft sharing.
5. They didn't follow the classmate's thinking and were instead thinking about their own thinking.
6. The task did not elicit much to wonder about.
7. They weren't ready to listen to someone else's thinking yet.
8. They weren't sure how to respond because they did not see anything to critique.

Siobahn landed on Conjectures 2 and 3, which was similar to my Conjecture 6. She said to me, "Maybe when I do this [rough draft sharing], it has to be with a task that challenges them a bit more—right in their zone of proximal development." I agreed that perhaps this task didn't present enough richness to lead to a larger discussion. She also said, "I have to be clear about what I want them to get out of the conversation." Although Siobahn knew what she wanted the preservice teachers to understand, perhaps this task and her questions did not elicit that thinking.

She noticed that she had more success with helping her students achieve exploratory thinking in another course that discussed properties of numeration systems. They had been working on understanding properties of numeration systems, such as additive, positional, multiplicative, place-valued, and having zero in various numeration systems. A tally numeration system is additive. The Egyptian numeration system is additive. The Babylonian numeration system is additive, positional, multiplicative, and place-valued, but it does not have a zero. The Hindu-Arabic numeration system has all of these properties. After this review, Siobhan posed the following question to the class: "What do you wonder about regarding these properties and possible numeration systems?" When they hesitated, Siobhan modeled a way of talking by saying, "For instance, I wonder if there is a number system that . . ."

Her students responded this time. One wondered, "Is there a numeration system that doesn't have an additive property, because all of the ones we looked at have that." Another said, "I wonder if there is a number system that is positional but not place-valued. I'm wondering if this is because I think that I don't understand the differences between the two." Wonderments like these felt more like rough draft thinking, so Siobahn was pleased that she offered a more open question that elicited honest, exploratory thinking from the students.

Although her conjectures made a lot of sense to me, I additionally landed on Conjecture 8: perhaps students were not sure how to share their thinking. What is there to say about a well-constructed diagram? According to Kazemi and Hintz (2014), an important principle of classroom discussions is that students benefit from understanding when and how to share their thinking. Maybe students were unfamiliar with how to share their thinking, considering that Siobahn's efforts to model ways of talking elicited more talk from the students. Maybe they needed support.

To help students know when and how to begin responding to a peer's thinking, we thought about introducing sentence starters. In my own teaching, I used to say, "What are your comments and questions about that?" It wasn't enough to get a conversation going. Once I introduced more specific sentence starters, I experienced a big shift in students' contributions.

We can use a variety of sentence starters. Here are some I have found to be helpful during mathematics classroom discussions, specifically Number Talks. This is not an exhaustive list:

SENTENCE STARTERS THAT CAN SUPPORT ROUGH DRAFT TALK

SHARE YOUR STRATEGY

The answer of ____________ makes sense because . . . (Explain)

I see it another way. (Explain)

DISCUSS SOMEONE ELSE'S STRATEGY

I noticed . . .

I agree because . . .

This makes sense because . . .

To add on . . .

I hear you saying that . . .

I don't know what you mean by . . .

This strategy is similar to / different from ____________ (enter name), because . . .

In Siobahn's classroom, her students—like most of ours!—might not be aware of ways to talk in nonevaluative ways about someone else's strategy. They might not know what to discuss or how to begin talking about others' thinking, especially when the thinking is correct. But there is always more to explore about someone's thinking.

We certainly do not want to talk about students' work only when it's incorrect. If we only spend time talking about someone's ideas when they're incorrect, then opening the floor after someone shares signals that their thinking is problematic. In other words, students will assume the math is wrong if we talk about it, which frames both talk and mistakes as negatives. Opening discussion about sound mathematical thinking helps us grow in our understanding and make new connections.

Siobahn saw potential in helping students know when and how to share. She decided to offer the following sentence starters in her rational number class:

- Your thinking is different from mine in this way . . .
- My thinking was similar in this way . . .

She also intended to think more about what she wanted students to think about and what sentence starters would help them get there. Siobahn was pleased that she decided on small changes to enact. She was also open to the notion that new dilemmas could arise through making these changes, even if they improved her classroom interactions about mathematics.

Siobahn's puzzle highlights the importance of choosing a task that involves a challenging concept worth exploring with rough draft thinking. Siobahn's story also illustrates that how the teacher poses questions to students when implementing a task can elicit more or less rough draft thinking. In the next chapter, we will go further into the role of task selection and implementation to engage students in rough draft thinking.

CHAPTER THREE

TASKS THAT PROVIDE OPPORTUNITIES TO COMMUNICATE TO LEARN

What are some features of math tasks that provide opportunities for students to communicate their thinking? For students to engage in rough draft math, they need spaces to share their initial ideas while they are in progress. They also need opportunities to revisit and revise those ideas so their thinking can continue to evolve. These spaces and opportunities begin with tasks that invite students to communicate their thinking about ideas. Consider the differences between the following tasks:

TWO CONTRASTING TASKS WITH DIFFERENT OPPORTUNITIES TO WORK ON UNDERSTANDING

Task A

Solve:

$x^2 - 4x - 5 = 0$

(Show your work.)

Task B

How can we find solution(s) to the quadratic function for each representation? What does it mean to find a solution for a quadratic function? (Communicate your thinking.)

Representation 1

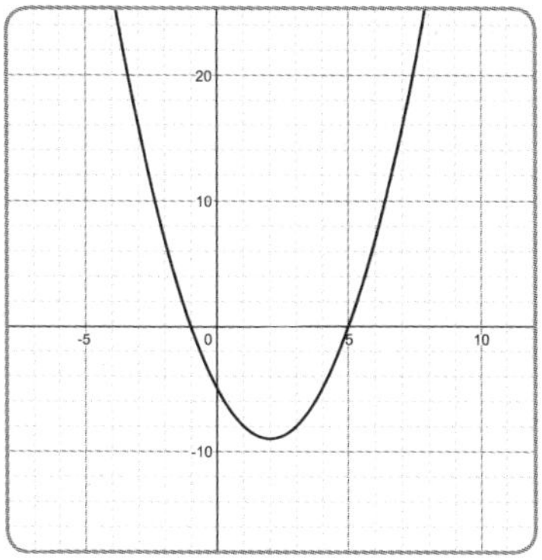

Representation 2

x	-3	-2	-1	0	1	2	3	4	5	6	7
y	16	7	0	-5	-8	-9	-8	-5	0	7	16

TABLE 3.1

I would want my students to be successful with both Task A and Task B, but Task B would be more likely to elicit students' thinking about a concept. Students are asked directly to write about their ideas about solutions. Some possible student ideas might be:

- "A solution is where the parabola crosses the x-axis. We can see it happening on the graph."
- "A solution is the answer (or answers) for x when the y-value is zero. We can look at the table where $y = 0$ to find the values for x."
- "This parabola has two solutions, but some parabolas have none and other parabolas might have only one solution."
- "A solution is called a root."

It is likely that many of these ideas will be generated, but no one student will have all of the ideas. After a number of initial ideas are solicited, students could be invited to write down their revised thinking on the meaning of a solution. Task B can foster a spirit of rough drafting because of the focus on ideas. However, perhaps the spirit of rough drafting could be applied to Task A, depending on how teachers and students interact around the task.

Both procedural fluency and conceptual understanding are important strands in developing proficiency in mathematics (Kilpatrick, Swafford, and Findell 2001). Task A is designed for students to calculate and execute procedures fluently. Students are expected to find two solutions: $x = -1$ and 5. Beyond writing out their work on Task A, the task is not written to invite students to think about solutions or what the solutions mean or to think about why their steps made sense.

Students are more likely to encounter a task like Task A in their math classes. The Education Trust conducted an analysis of more than 1,800 middle-grades assignments from more than ninety math courses from twelve middle schools in six districts across the country (Dysarz 2018). This analysis revealed that only 32 percent of mathematics assignments asked students to communicate or justify their thinking. Instead, most mathematics assignments were answer-focused. To support students' ongoing sense-making, we must select and implement tasks that create space for further thinking. I see Task B as supporting communicating to develop understanding of a concept.

If we assign tasks that look mostly like Task A, we can still pose questions to students that invite rough draft thinking. When Annie Fetter, formerly of the Math Forum, spoke at the Colorado Council of Teachers of Mathematics annual meeting in 2017, she said that if you want students to talk about ideas, you need to ask students about ideas. We might usually ask, *What's the answer to problem number 7?* But we elicit more ideas from students by saying instead, *Tell me something about problem number 7*. If we invite students to talk about their ideas rather than their answers or their steps for calculating, students will have more opportunities to develop their thinking. To invite thinking on Task A, I might begin the discussion by asking, *What makes sense to you about this task?*

I could also imagine inviting rough draft thinking in other ways when implementing Task A. This task can be solved by multiple strategies: factoring, the quadratic formula, completing the square, or graphing the function and finding where the parabola crossed the x-axis. We could select different student-generated strategies (perhaps a factoring strategy and a graphing strategy). Then, we could ask students to share, compare, and contrast their strategies to explain how they see their answers in each strategy. Students could grow in their understandings about solutions for quadratic functions through comparing strategies. Alternatively, we could ask students a follow-up question to reflect on Task A: *Does this quadratic equation have one solution, two solutions, or none? Why would it make sense for this equation to have that number of solutions? How might a graph or a table help us make sense of the number of solutions?* These reflection questions push students to think about the meaning of a solution for a quadratic function.

In this chapter, we'll think about how task selection and implementation can foster opportunities for students to think about concepts and communicate their thinking. Certain tasks provide more spaces for students to deepen their mathematical understandings through rough draft thinking. If the task doesn't already provide opportunities for students to think and communicate, we can open up more thinking opportunities as we implement the task.

Features of Tasks That Invite Rough Draft Thinking

Based on my explorations, I have encountered some features of tasks that support rough draft thinking, but I haven't exhausted all the possibilities. So far, I have noticed that these kinds of tasks invite students to communicate to learn:

FEATURES OF TASKS THAT INVITE ROUGH DRAFT THINKING

- Tasks that ask students to explain their thinking about a concept
- Tasks that have more than one good answer
- Tasks that can be solved with more than one good strategy
- Tasks that ask students to predict and then test and revise predictions

If I encounter a task that does not already have one of these features, I wonder how the task can be modified to add in one of these features during implementation.

Tasks That Ask Students to Explain Their Thinking About a Concept

If rough draft thinking is communicating to continue to develop understandings, then we want to give students opportunities to talk or write about an idea or concept. Task B (see Table 3.1) invites students to reflect on what constitutes a solution for a quadratic function. Thinking about the solution as it appears in multiple representations provides a chance for students to think about the meaning of a solution to the function.

We can take a task and leverage it to make sense out of concepts (or not). I observed two different seventh-grade classrooms discussing the same *Walkathon* problem from *Connected Mathematics Project* (Lappan et al. 2002). One teacher engaged students in rough draft thinking about a concept and the other teacher invited the students to talk about calculating (Jansen 2008).

Here is the task that the two classes discussed. (Mrs. Evans's and Ms. Carson's names are pseudonyms.)

WALKATHON TASK

Ms. Chang says that some sponsors might ask the students to suggest a pledge amount. The class wants to agree on how much they ask for.

- Leanne says that each sponsor should pay $10 regardless of how far a person walks.
- Gilberto says that $2 per kilometer would be better because it would bring in more money.
- Alana points out that if they ask for too much money, not as many people will want to be sponsors. She suggests that they ask each sponsor for $5 plus 50 cents per kilometer.

For each pledge plan:

1. Make a table showing the amount of money a sponsor would owe if a student walked distances from 1 to 6 kilometers.
2. Graph the three pledge plans on the same coordinate axis. Use a different color for each plan.

Write an equation that can be used to calculate the amount of money a sponsor owes, given the total distance the student walks. What are the independent and dependent variables?

★ What Makes a Relationship Linear?

In Mrs. Evans's classroom, students were repeatedly asked to justify whether they believed the relationship between two variables was linear. This was a relevant conversation because situations like Alana's plan were new for the students. The graph did not start at the origin, so it presented a conundrum for the students: it did not have a graph exactly like the other linear relationships they had encountered. To determine whether it was linear, students in Mrs. Evans's class made connections between the problem context and what they already knew about linear relationships when discussing Alana's plan.

> **Mrs. Evans:** *Steve.*
>
> **Steve**: *Okay, thank you. See, didn't she, didn't someone give her a pledge for five dollars?*
>
> **Mrs. Evans:** *That's what she's saying, yeah.*
>
> **Steve:** *If someone gave her a pledge for five dollars, that's just like the zero, you know?*

Steve justified that Alana's plan was a linear relationship by relating the initial five-dollar pledge to where you would cross the *y*-axis on a graph, which was at the origin in the other relationships, "just like the zero." Steve engaged in rough draft thinking about whether this relationship was linear as he related his prior understandings about linear functions to his understanding of Alana's plan.

The class continued to discuss whether Alana's plan was a linear relationship, and Molly made the connection to prior linear situations that had unit rates.

> **Mrs. Evans:** *Okay, Molly, other thoughts.*
>
> **Molly:** *For Alana, the reason why I thought it was, um, linear, I don't know if it is, because a unit rate is when it's at one, and you really shouldn't count the zero, because it's really not at that, you know what I mean, because, like, one kilometer is like her unit rate, that's* (fifty cents) *what she gets per kilometer, so that's why.*

We can hear the uncertainty in Molly's talk ("I don't know if it is . . ."), which suggests that Molly was in a rough draft thinking space. A practice had previously emerged in this classroom such that students agreed that they could find the unit rate represented on the graph for the y-value when the x-value was 1. However, previously, students had only experienced relationships when the graph went through the origin (0, 0). When students encountered a situation that did not go through the origin, the new situation challenged their strategies for finding unit rates. Molly determined that Alana's relationship was similar to the linear relationships they had encountered previously by going back to the problem context to point out a unit rate.

It was Mrs. Evans's choice to ask the class whether these *Walkathon* pledge plans were linear. The written task did not ask the students to consider whether the plans were linear. Asking the students to reflect on the meaning of linear functions generated a larger conceptual conversation about the pledge plans. Students made connections between representations on this problem and previous problems from the unit on linear functions.

★ What's the Next Step?

When Ms. Carson implemented the same problem, she spent more time on procedural aspects of the task, such as asking students to describe how to calculate values for the dependent variable in the *Walkathon* problem.

> **Ms. Carson:** *What about Alana* (how much money would she collect after walking eight kilometers)*?*
>
> **Max:** *Nine dollars.*
>
> **Ms. Carson:** *How did you get nine dollars?*
>
> **Max:** *Well, she started with five dollars, and then she did fifty cents times eight, and then I got four, and I just added.*
>
> **Ms. Carson:** *Okay, good.*

Her students spent more time talking about how they calculated and less time communicating to understand a concept.

★ Why Does That Step Make Sense?

When Mrs. Evans's class talked about answers to the task as written, such as writing equations for each pledge plan, students talked about not just what they did but why the steps made sense. Jim nominated an equation of $y = 10x$ to represent Leanne's plan. Molly disagreed.

> **Molly:** *Um, the 10, Jim's ($y = 10x$) wouldn't work, because that's saying for every kilometer that you go, you add 10 more. That's not going to work.*
>
> **Ms. Evans:** *So, you don't like this one? I'm not sure that everyone at that back table is listening. Molly is saying she doesn't like this one. Say it one more time, because I'm not sure it's all been heard.*
>
> **Molly:** *Because, 10, it's saying that for every kilometer you go, you're adding 10 more, so if you go 2, you're gonna have 20, and it's really only 10.*

To make sense out of why she thought Jim's equation wouldn't work, Molly appealed to the quantities in the problem to make sense of what was happening. She did not talk about calculating; she did not say that if you put in 2 for x, you would get 20.

Whether or not the task is written to invite students to think about concepts, we can implement a task so students can think about concepts. If linear relationships have a unit rate, where do you see the rate in this situation? If linear relationships cross the y-axis at a certain point, where do we see the y-intercept in the story, graph, or table? Now that we see a graph, a story problem, or a relationship between two values in a table, what do we look for to decide whether that relationship is linear? If we ask students to explain how they calculated, we can press students to explain why those steps make sense (or not). If we consider what concepts we want students to understand, we can foster communicating to learn through rough draft thinking.

Tasks That Have More Than One Good Answer

Tasks with more than one good answer foster discussions about mathematics and opportunities to revise thinking. For example, students could write a story problem to represent what is happening in a graph or an equation. Consider a story that represents the graph in Figure 3.1.

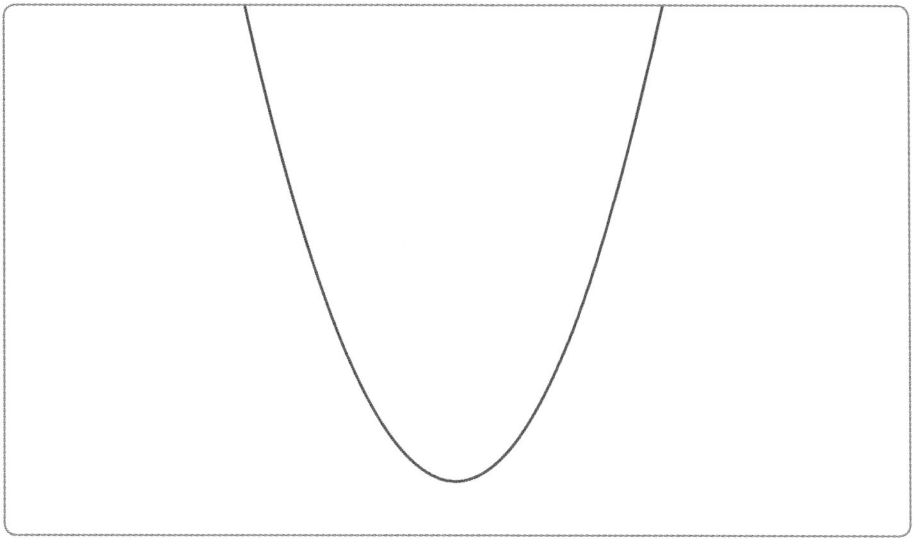

Figure 3.1
What story might this graph represent?

A student might say that she likes hot coffee or cold coffee, but she dislikes lukewarm coffee. In this story, the vertical axis represents the level of happiness or enjoyment, and the horizontal axis measures the temperature of the coffee. Another student might think about the graph in terms of a heavy object on wheels, rolling toward a person. She applies a constant force on the tire to slow it down. She continues to apply a steady force, and eventually, it stops and starts moving in the other direction from which it came. As it moves away from her, she continues to apply the same constant force, and the object continues to pick up speed, moving away from her. The graph could represent a distance time–graph, where distance is measured on the *y*-axis as decreasing as the object moves toward the woman and increasing as it moves away from the woman. There are also other stories that align with the graph, and the class could discuss whether and why stories fit.

We can ask students to write story problems about equations as well as graphs. For example, consider $1\frac{1}{4} \div \frac{1}{8} = ?$ Some possible story problems students could write follow.

POSSIBLE STORY PROBLEM SITUATIONS TO REPRESENT $1\frac{1}{4} \div \frac{1}{8} = ?$

Sylvester bought a bungee cord that measured $1\frac{1}{4}$ yards. If he divides it into cords that are each $\frac{1}{8}$ yard, how many pieces will he have?

Jordan had $1\frac{1}{4}$ cups of lemonade, which filled $\frac{1}{8}$ of a thermos for the soccer team. How many cups of lemonade would have filled the entire thermos?

Both of these stories represent the equation. Comparing and contrasting them provides an opportunity to think about the operation of division in two ways. In the first problem, repeatedly subtracting the divisor of $\frac{1}{8}$ from the dividend of $1\frac{1}{4}$ to find how many copies of $\frac{1}{8}$ yard fit into $1\frac{1}{4}$ yards represents the *measurement* meaning of division. In the second problem, finding the amount in one group (one full thermos) given an amount ($1\frac{1}{4}$ cups) in a partial number of groups ($\frac{1}{8}$ of a thermos), represents the *partitive* meaning of division.

It's likely that many students will create stories that do not represent the equation: *Hannah has $1\frac{1}{4}$ gallons of water that she wants to share with eight friends. How much water did each friend get?* This story problem actually represents $1\frac{1}{4} \div 8 = ?$, but it is a common mistake students make when encountering problems like $1\frac{1}{4} \div \frac{1}{8} = ?$ In addition, students might write *Julien had $1\frac{1}{4}$ gallons of water. He spilled $\frac{1}{8}$ of it. How many gallons of water did he spill?* This story aligns better with $\frac{1}{8} \times 1\frac{1}{4} = ?$ Drawing pictures of the solutions to multiple story problems can help students make sense of which stories align with the division number sentence and which stories represent other operations. Students can then revise their thinking about division with fractions.

For tasks like these, there are many possible ways to think about mathematical relationships, and there is not one single correct answer. Eliciting a range of potentially correct stories that represent the graph or equation invites conversation about mathematical ideas and principles underlying key features in the stories. In the coffee story, students can discuss how the quantity of happiness level depends on the level of the temperature and observe the relationships between them visually on the graph. They can contrast the coffee story with the rolling object story to understand how functional relationships between two quantities vary in ways that are represented by the graph. In the division story, students could make sense of different ways that division behaves as an operation. In each task, once students write one story that aligns with the equation or graph, they could try to write another one or compare their story with a classmate's. The class could discuss and identify common features of representative stories and explore how the features align with the graph or equation.

When students work on tasks with more than one good answer, more students' ideas can be elevated as valuable and correct. Students experience that doing mathematics involves reasoning and justifying. Students' thinking can be revised after seeking to understand their peers' thinking. If students are satisfied with correct answers and do not feel a desire to develop alternative strategies to solve a problem, this is a sign that our lessons need to invite thinking about more than answers.

Tasks That Can Be Solved with More Than One Good Strategy

Some problems have single, correct answers and still invite rough draft thinking and discourse. These problems generate multiple solution strategies that can be compared and contrasted to develop further understandings. Essentially, any problem that students can solve in more than one way expands thinking and discussing about mathematics. To help students feel free to see mathematical situations in more than one way, routines can be useful.

★ Contemplate-then-Calculate

Let's consider a routine called "Contemplate-then-Calculate" (Kelmanik, Lucenta, and Creighton 2016). When implementing Contemplate-then-Calculate, the teacher flashes up the image relatively quickly. Students contemplate ways of seeing the image that could help them calculate. Then they share with a partner to explain how they saw the image, which portions or sections they saw, in what order, and how viewing the image in this way helped them determine the total number of objects. Through sharing, students develop new ways of seeing structure. The teacher then shares the image again, and the class spends time talking about various ways of seeing the image and what might be mathematically important in what they see.

Figure 3.2
How do you see the number of eggs in the image?

In my undergraduate course for preservice teachers about pedagogical methods for teaching mathematics in elementary grades, we shared our thinking about Figure 3.2 using the Contemplate-then-Calculate routine. The image was projected along with two sentence starters to promote interaction around students' thinking (Table 3.2).

SENTENCE STARTERS FOR CONTEMPLATE-THEN-CALCULATE

Presenter	Audience
I noticed . . . so I . . . I know . . . so I . . .	They noticed . . . so they . . . They knew . . . so they . . .

TABLE 3.2

After their partner conversations, the preservice teachers shared what they noticed in the large group.

Anne: *If you split it in half, these images mirror each other. So this makes an H and this makes an H. I saw that this half was three-by-three, so that's nine, and two were missing. That would be seven. Seven times two is fourteen.*

Mandy: *Can you comment on what Anne noticed?*

Becca: *She noticed that the two halves were symmetrical, so she could just look at one side. And then multiplying it by two, she could find the answer.*

Callie: *I actually started out like she did, but I didn't actually think about it as a three-by-three minus two. So, I regrouped it in my head, ended up leaving that behind.*

Mandy: *So, what did you do differently?*

Callie: *Oh, I halved it, and then I was like, never mind.* (She and the class all laugh.)

Mandy: *How did you go after that?*

Callie: *I noticed the three, six, three, and then plus two.* (Callie came up to point at what she saw, which was one column of three, two columns of three, another column of three, and then the other two single eggs.)

Mandy: *What are your comments about what Callie saw?*

Dori: *That's exactly what I did: three, six, nine, twelve.*

Mandy: *Can you come show us?*

Dori: (points at each column): *Three, six, nine, twelve, and then* (points at the last two dots) *thirteen and fourteen.*

Mandy: *Oh! You skip-counted by threes? Is that what you're saying?*

Dori: *Yes.*

Mandy: *Cool! Elle?*

Elle: *That's kind of how I saw it. I saw that there were four columns of three, so I did three times four is twelve and then thirteen, fourteen.*

Mandy: *Other ways of chunking this or figuring out how to see it?*

Felicity: *I did six times three because there are three rows of six and then subtracted four.*

Mandy: *So you looked at what?*

Felicity: *I guess if there were none missing. I did that. Then I subtracted.*

Mandy: *You found the whole area, a three-by-six array or a six-by-three array, and took out four from there?*

Felicity: *Yeah.*

Mandy: *Other ways of seeing it?*

Gina: *I looked at it as three groups of six and two those of three groups had some missing. Like there's six minus two. Then there's a group of six. And then another group of six minus two.*

Mandy: *Looks like another case of seeing what full sets are there and taking out missing parts.*

Hannah: *I saw those groups of six, too, but I moved two of the middle* circles (from the columns in the middle) *over to fill up one group to make six. I moved two more middle circles* (from the columns in the middle) *over to make that other group six and get twelve all together. Then thirteen, fourteen, with the last two left* (from the columns in the middle).

Mandy: *So what do we think about the differences between how Hannah and Gina thought about it? Can someone comment on that?*

Jessica: *Gina counted the missing circles and subtracted them out of the possible total. Hannah filled in empty spots.*

Gina: *Scooting them over helped me see it.*

Mandy: *Any other ways?*

Karen: *The two columns going down in the middle, I knew that was six. If I looked at the side, that's four. And six and four is ten. There's four on the other side. Ten plus four is fourteen.*

Mandy: *Making tens! What else?*

Lisa: *I went across the rows. The middle row is six, then the top row with that now makes ten. Bringing in the bottom row makes fourteen.*

Mandy: *Did anyone see a way that they hadn't thought about before?*

After this conversation, I asked the class to write a reflection using this sentence starter: *Noticing* ____________ *helped me count because* __________. (All sentence starters I used for supporting discussion and reflection were from Kelemanik et al. [2016]).

The underlying goal of this routine is to help students learn to pay attention to mathematical structure, which aligns with the seventh Standard for Mathematical Practice in the Common Core State Standards: Look for and make use of structure. The notion of structure in this routine relates to ways of seeing relationships and engaging in multiple ways of seeing. We can calculate more efficiently using these structures. Through Contemplate-then-Calculate, students are asked to count quickly by chunking or changing the form in what they see and connecting to mathematics they know.

The process of identifying a structure supports generalizing patterns. Consider dot patterns that grow, such as the one in Figure 3.3. Examining the structure of the first figure (arranged like the eggs) allows for under-

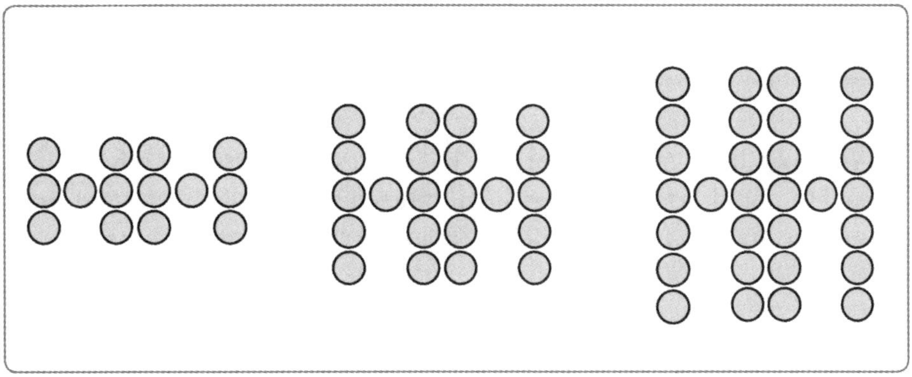

Figure 3.3
Growing pattern that builds on the egg carton image's structure

standing ways of seeing how the pattern is growing from Shape 1 to Shape 2 to Shape 3. Then, once we see the structure in how the pattern is growing, we can predict, for instance, how many circles will be in the forty-third pattern. Visualizing structure supports engaging in mathematical thinking, such as generalizing.

Rough draft thinking happens during this routine when learners brainstorm how they can chunk or change the representation that they see. Such initial ideas are *exploratory insights*. Then learners share what they notice with others, which provides opportunities to *revise* how someone could chunk or change the representation to calculate more quickly. The multiple instances of contemplation built into the Contemplate-then-Calculate routine align well with the notion of rough draft thinking.

A routine such as Contemplate-then-Calculate can support students' use of rough draft thinking to understand ideas if at least two opportunities are built in:

CRITERIA FOR ROUTINES THAT SUPPORT ROUGH DRAFT THINKING

1. **Students are asked to share *unfinished, in-progress thinking*, which they are invited to explore and brainstorm together.**
2. **Students are explicitly asked to *revise their thinking* through chances to reflect on their initial brainstorms, change their thinking, and reflect on changes in their thinking.**

Multiple instructional routines have these opportunities built into them, but not all routines have them. If teachers implement routines with these opportunities, they can engage students in rough draft thinking.

Tasks that Ask Students to Predict, Then Test and Revise Predictions

When students make initial predictions before solving a task, rough draft thinking takes place because students eventually revisit and revise their predictions. Students take a stance, and then students justify their stance with data gathered through further mathematical investigation. Modeling tasks are opportunities to engage in rough draft thinking.

★ Ice Cubed: Revising Initial Predictions with More Thorough Mathematical Justifications

In the problem *Ice Cubed*, from the Mathalicious website (mathalicious.com/ice-cubed), students generate and explore conjectures to investigate relationships between surface area and volume. I launch this task with a *Would you rather?* posed to the class. Would they rather have a glass with a single ice cube (such as one 6 cm × 6 cm × 6 cm ice cube) or a glass with multiple ice cubes made up of the same volume of water (such as twenty-seven 2 cm × 2 cm × 2 cm ice cubes)? Instead of giving the numerical data of the size of the cubes, I display a picture of a single ice cube and multiple ice cubes (Figure 3.4) when asking which they would rather have.

Figure 3.4
Which would you rather have?

Students are invited to share reasons for choosing either type of ice cube:

- They would rather have the smaller cubes because they like the sound of ice clinking in the glass or they like to chew ice.

- The smaller set of cubes would be better because they make the drink colder more quickly.
- They don't want the ice to hit them in the face, so they don't want the larger cubes.
- The larger ice cube wouldn't melt as quickly, which would be better because the drink would be less watery.

Students eventually come up with the conjecture that the single ice cube melts more slowly, and they have differing opinions about whether they prefer this option. They may even begin to conjecture that surface area matters, comparing more surface area (multiple smaller cubes) with less surface area (single larger cube). Then students can work through the worksheet from Mathalicious on which they are invited to generate data to investigate how much more slowly the single cube would melt compared to various smaller sets of ice cubes.

It is also helpful to discuss constraints and assumptions to make progress on the task. For instance, the Mathalicious worksheet establishes that the same liquid (lemonade, of course) is in both glasses, and it starts at room temperature. Assumptions have to be made about melting rates to explore how quickly cubes melt when they have different side lengths.

When students revise their thinking on problems like *Ice Cubed*, they do not necessarily change their stances. This task happens to be an example of another problem that has more than one correct answer. Students' initial preferences or predictions of what they prefer might not change. But students' rationales for their stances can become more thoroughly justified by data that they generate through working on the problem. Their understandings of key mathematical concepts—in this case, surface area as it relates to volume—can also become more nuanced through working on the problem.

★ World as 100 People: Predicting and Revising Thinking About the World Through Mathematics

Students can also use mathematics to predict and revise their predictions about the world around them. Through their writing, Lynette Guzmán and Jeffrey Craig (2019) introduced me to a task about the *World as 100 People*. In this problem, students initially reflect on what the world would be like, as a village, if the population of the entire world was scaled down to one hundred people. Then they revise their thinking based on data.

Students would be asked to predict, if the world were one hundred people, how many people would . . . have a shelter, have safe water to drink, be able to access the Internet, have a college degree, be able to read and write, have cell phones, and any other aspects of experience in the world. One strategy to use when eliciting predictions would be to have students share their thinking anonymously and display the range of predictions. When eliciting predictions, it's important to emphasize that the goal is not to be "right" the first time. Instead, through our efforts to predict, we hope to surface our assumptions about the world.

After predicting, students could be provided with data about the world. They could reflect on what they notice and wonder about the data. What is surprising? Why? What stories do these data tell us? Students could then engage in mathematical explorations, given the total number of people in the world. They could find out how many people actually have access to safe water, for instance. Students draw on both mathematical concepts and ideas about the world while reflecting on predictions in this task.

Guzmán and Craig also recommend an extension task: choosing a country and researching what that country would be like as one hundred people. Students create representations to illustrate their countries as one hundred people. They discuss their strategies to create their representations, as well as surprises about different countries' data. Students and teachers alike might realize that our predictions are centered closely on our own experiences.

Task Implementation to Invite Rough Draft Thinking

So far, in this chapter, we have looked at tasks structured to invite rough draft thinking. Even with tasks that are not inherently designed to encourage rough draft thinking, we can still incorporate implementation practices that invite continued development of thinking. For a task that emphasizes procedural fluency, students' thinking would evolve if they compared strategies or were asked to reflect about the concepts in the problem. Two additional implementation strategies have supported my students with engaging rough draft thinking: (1) cutting the scaffolds or questions and (2) using Bet Lines to activate thinking and sense-making while launching a task. Therefore, we have four ways we can modify a task to implement rough draft thinking.

MODIFICATIONS TO A TASK TO IMPLEMENT ROUGH DRAFT THINKING

- Comparing and contrasting strategies for solving a problem
- Reflecting on the concepts in a problem
- Cutting scaffolds or questions from a task, then noticing and wondering
- Launching a task using Bet Lines to activate thinking and sense-making

I have already explored the first two modifications previously in this chapter, so I will next reflect on the latter two ways of modifying and implementing tasks to promote rough draft thinking. These are not the only ways a teacher could modify tasks through implementation, but these implementation strategies have been useful for me.

Cutting Scaffolds or Questions from a Task, Then Noticing and Wondering

When we encounter a task that feels somewhat closed, sometimes we can modify it and open it up by removing scaffolds. Textbook tasks often have many substeps included in the problem, which end up doing the mathematical thinking of decomposing a complex task into its less complex parts for students. Taking away these scaffolds can enable rough draft thinking because we are then, as Dan Meyer (2010) has said, *rebuilding* a problem in a way that supports math reasoning and problem solving.

One way to modify a task is to eliminate the text and the question. Show students the visual diagram that the task is based on and ask students what they notice (Fetter 2011; Ray-Riek 2013). I have experimented with this possibility in my mathematics methods course for future elementary teachers. For example, the mathematical goal during one class was to view area as covering a two-dimensional plane in terms of square units, which enhances and extends a view of area as calculating length × width. When students think about calculating length × width, they do not always visualize covering a plane with square units. To promote this idea, I wanted my students to work with areas of irregular polygons and to generate a range of strategies for decomposing the polygons into shapes for which they could more easily calculate area and then recompose to find the total area of the irregular polygon. I started by selecting the task in Figure 3.5, which was an eighth-grade item from the National Assessment of Educational Progress (NAEP) in 2005.

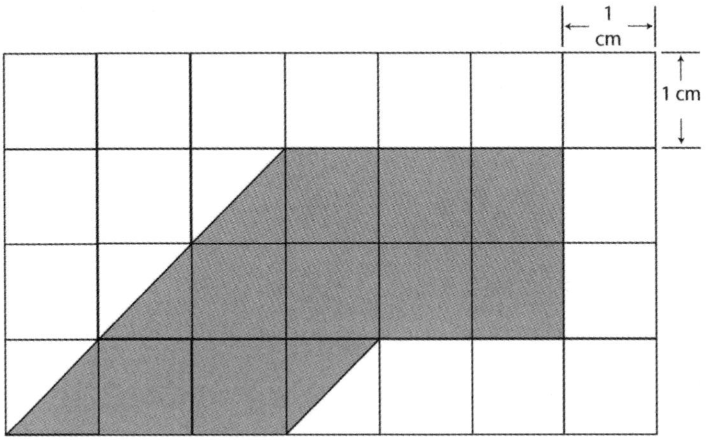

What is the area of the shaded figure?

A. 9 square centimeters

B. 11 square centimeters

C. 13 square centimeters

D. 14 square centimeters

Figure 3.5
NAEP 2005 multiple-choice task: area of an irregular polygon

I then modified the task by displaying only the visual diagram of the irregular polygon (Figure 3.6). I cut out the question and the multiple-choice options. I said to the class, "Look at this image and think about what you're noticing."

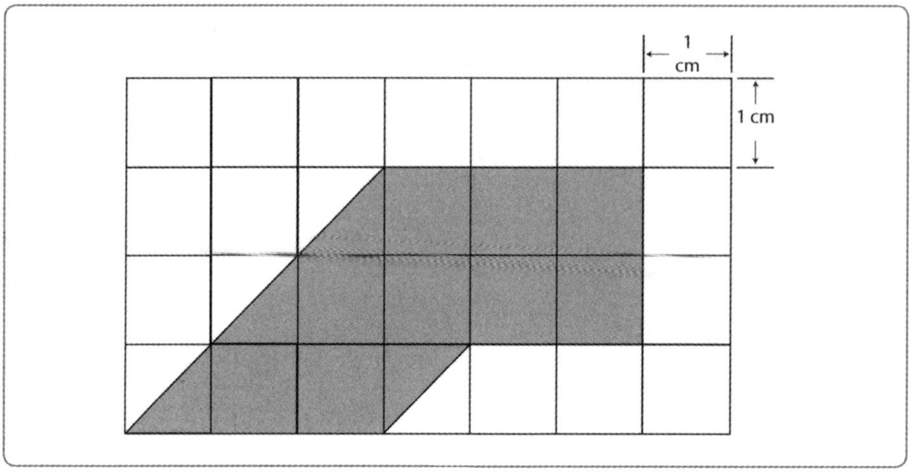

Figure 3.6
What do you notice about this diagram?

After some wait time, students shared what they noticed.

> **Madison:** *I noticed that some of the boxes are completely shaded. Some of the boxes are half shaded.*
>
> **Lauren:** *When I looked at it, I immediately saw three shapes. I saw a big triangle, a rectangle, and a small triangle.* (I had Lauren come to the document camera and point to these three shapes within the irregular polygon.)
>
> **Holly:** *One of these unit squares is one square centimeter. You can tell because the width and the length are both a centimeter.* (Holly came up to the document camera to point this out.)
>
> **Olivia:** *I noticed that four of the boxes were only covered in half, which was, when we're trying to compare, would be two full boxes.* (Olivia came up to the document camera to point out how she saw this.) *I was saying, like, these two would make a whole* (points to two halves) *and these two would make a whole* (points to two other halves) *when we were trying to see, like, how many squares were colored compared to the ones not.*
>
> **Lauren:** *I noticed that there's a shape colored in within a bigger shape that's not colored in. So, if we wanted to find how much of it is colored*

in, we could always find the total number of cubes (square units). *We could always use that to help us to find out what's colored in by maybe subtracting.*

I then displayed the diagram with the prompt, *What is the area of the shaded figure?* I asked the class to determine the area, in terms of square units, by considering what people noticed. Rough draft talk happened when discussing this image because my students explored a number of initial brainstorms about how to view the image in terms of its area. No student completely solved the problem before we started sharing out ideas. Each way of seeing could provide insight to get started on the problem. Students could revise their initial way of seeing after exposure to another way of seeing the problem.

When students shared how they found their areas of 11 square centimeters, they discussed how they applied these ways of seeing the area of the irregular polygons.

Chloe used Olivia's strategy of taking half boxes and combining them to make full boxes (Figure 3.7). "So, I kind of started by counting up the ones, the full boxes that I already knew, so I did 1, 2, 3, 4, 5, 6, 7, and then

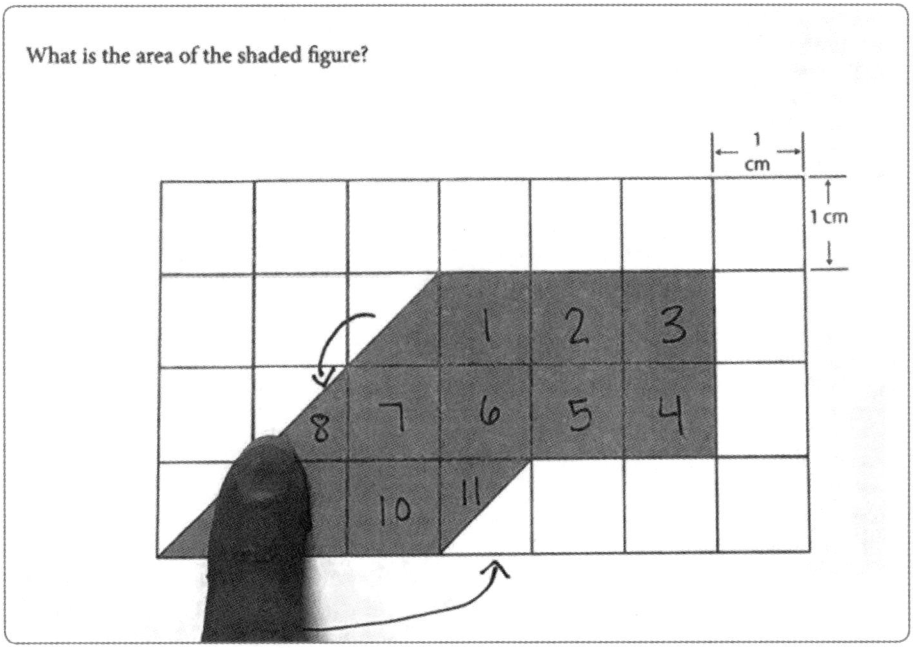

Figure 3.7
Chloe's way of seeing the area

I got to a half. So, I took the half from the beginning, and I put an arrow to the other one just to show that I was putting them together. That made eight. And then I skipped this half and I did nine, ten, and I got to another half, so I moved this one over to make another full square. So, I got eleven full squares all together."

Leah used the strategy of taking the larger shape and breaking it into smaller shapes (Figure 3.8). She said, "I found this rectangle here, and that was six. And I also moved these over (small half squares) to complete these two (to fill in the parts of the remaining triangle section) to make them into full squares, so I knew I had five there. So I could combine my two

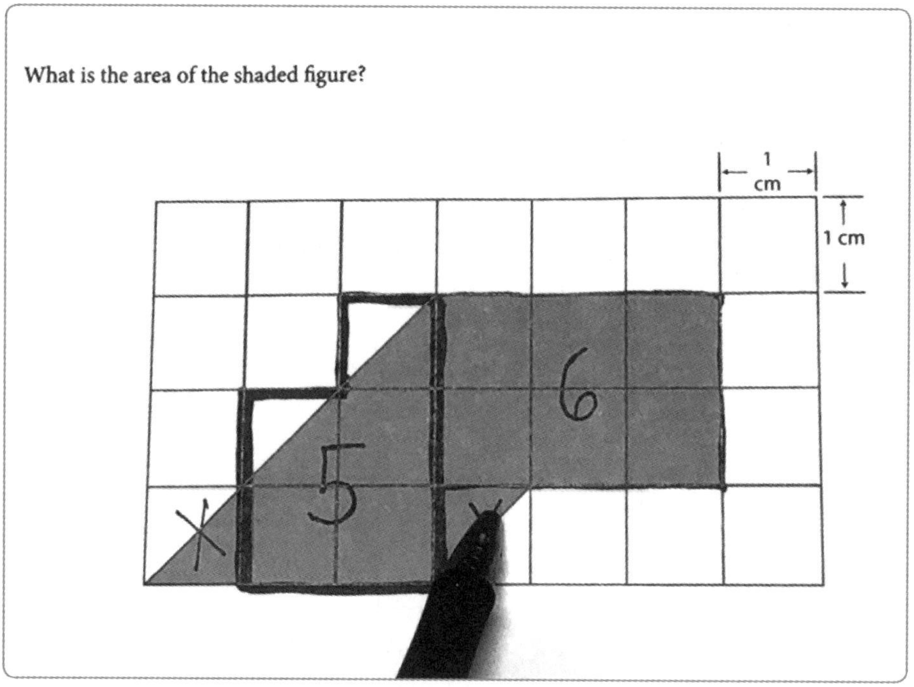

Figure 3.8
Leah's way of seeing the area

shapes."

I noticed that the class wasn't picking up on an important idea from Lauren's perspective, of finding the area of a larger space and then subtracting to find the area of a smaller space.

I drew a rectangle (square in this case), and asked, "How can this rectangle help us find the area of just that triangle?" (Figure 3.9). I asked the class to turn and talk to one another about this idea, so they could extend their current thinking as a way of revising.

Aimee said, "We saw that it (square) was three by three, so it's nine. And then half of it would be four and a half."

The students then continued to solve for the areas of multiple irregular shapes and came up to discuss how they looked at the image to help them determine the area.

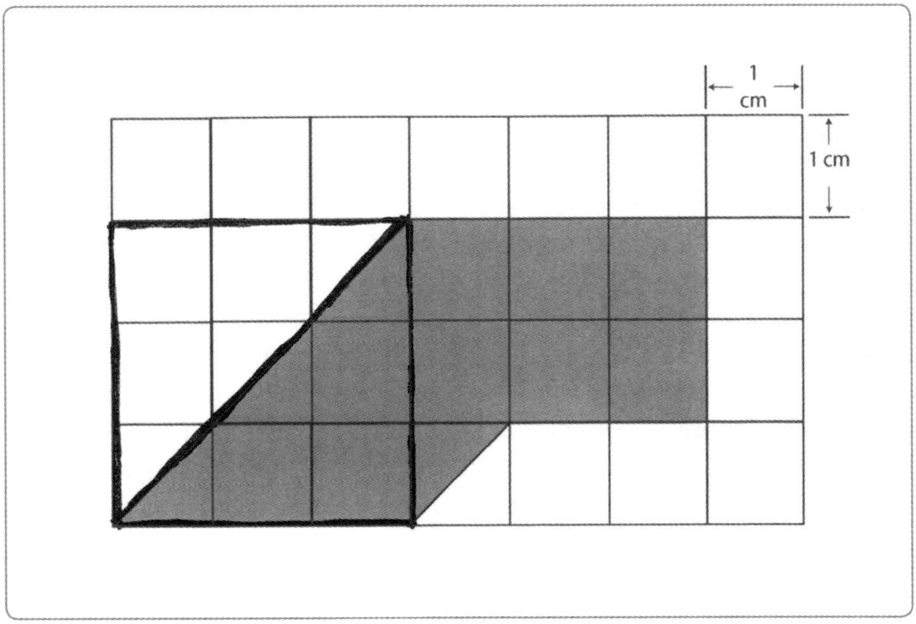

Figure 3.9
Connecting to Lauren's way of seeing the area

What I noticed, instructionally, is that by removing the directions from the task and showing the image of the irregular polygon first, encouraged my students to notice aspects of the shape itself. From that noticing, strategies then emerged: combining halves of boxes to make a full box; decomposing the irregular shape into smaller, more familiar shapes; situating the irregular shape within a larger, more familiar shape. I could see students applying what classmates noticed to find the area. Brainstorming during exploratory talk led to inspiration for strategies. Removing directions and asking students to reflect on a mathematical situation before solving opens up rough draft thinking that can support engagement in problem solving.

Launching a Task Using Bet Lines to Activate Thinking and Sense-Making

Bet Lines is an approach for launching a story problem task by asking students to make predictions about the problem itself (Dick et al. 2016). This approach is used to scaffold students' understanding of the task itself. Teachers gradually reveal parts of the story problem up to key stopping points, ask students what they think about what they just read, and then ask students to predict what comes next in the problem. There are no right or wrong predictions, but some predictions are more helpful for making sense of the mathematics in the situation.

I have preservice teachers rehearse before teaching students in kindergarten through twelve classrooms to practice teaching and revise their instruction. My preservice teachers were placed in pairs in a classroom, so they launched this problem in a coteaching structure. Their "students" for the rehearsal were their peers. My undergraduates rehearsed using Bet Lines to launch a problem for their fifth-grade students. These preservice teachers, Holly and Ellie, decided to change a problem in their curriculum materials to feature a particular student in their class, Quinton, who was known for his long hair. They displayed part of the problem in writing on the document camera: *Quinton's hair is 24 inches long and grows at a constant rate.*

> **Holly:** *Today, we're going to be looking at different patterns and ways to input data from a table onto a coordinate plane. The first thing that we're going to do is go through a problem step by step as a class. And I don't want you to think about the answer right away. I want you to think about the information given, the context, and making a bet about what could logically come next in the problem based on what we know so far.*
>
> **Ellie:** *As we move through the problem, I want you all to think about reasonable suggestions that can help us solve the problem. We want you to respect your classmate's bets. There are no wrong answers. All participation is appreciated. So, when you're answering these, we want you to phrase your prediction in the form of "I bet . . ."*

Holly: *So, we're going to start off with the beginning part of the problem. Quinton's hair is 24 inches long and grows at a constant rate. What do we know in this problem? What do we know so far?*

Stephanie: *His hair is 24 inches long already.* (Holly writes *24 inches* down.)

Holly: *And what does it mean for something to grow at a constant rate?*

Melanie: *It grows the same amount in a certain amount of time. Constant growth over a certain amount of time.* (Holly writes *constant rate: grows same amount in period of time.*)

Holly: *Can we take some bets on what part of the problem could come next? Think about what information we need to know, where to go from here.*

Chloe: *I bet it's going to tell us what the constant rate is.* (Holly writes, *What is the rate?*)

Holly: *Does anyone else have any ideas? Lauren?*

Lauren: *I bet the problem will tell us how long his hair is now or after some time has passed.* (Holly writes, *How long his hair grows to be.*)

Holly: *Anyone else have a bet they'd like to make? Madison?*

Madison: *I bet they'll say how long the period of time is.* (Holly writes, *What period of time?*)

Ellie: *So these are all great bets. I'm going to reveal what's next. So, every month, his hair grows one-half inch. Do we have any explanations of what this means?*

Erin: *The constant rate would be of one-half of an inch per month.* (Ellie writes, *constant rate* = $\frac{1}{2}$ *inch per month.*)

Ellie: *Does anyone else have any explanations? No? How about bets? Can we make bets about what comes next?*

> **Erin:** *I bet they tell us how much time goes by, and we have to find out how long his hair is. I bet they tell us the amount of months and want us to find how long his hair is in total.* (Ellie writes, *Bet: Amount of months* ⇨ *how long hair is in total.*)
>
> **Hannah:** *I bet they'll tell us how long his hair was at the start and ask us how long his hair has been growing.*
>
> **Ellie:** *Okay. Length and the start and then?*
>
> **Hannah:** *How long it's been growing for.*
>
> **Lauren:** *I bet they'll tell us how many months we're tracking his hair growth.*
>
> (Holly reveals the next question: *How long will Quinton's hair be after one year?*)
>
> **Holly:** *So, the next part of the question is,* How long will Quinton's hair be after one year? *It turns out that Erin's bet was correct.*

A key moment when soliciting students' predictions is encouraging speculation in ways that do not feel like fishing for the correct prediction. The preservice teachers attempted to invite a range of predictions by writing down all of the ideas offered. Perhaps they could have elicited more rather than moving on once they received the prediction they wanted, however. Holly continued:

> **Holly:** *We are given the time period that we are tracking, and it is asking for how long his hair is in total. What new information does this part of the problem give us?*
>
> **Sam:** *How long his hair has been growing.* (Holly writes this.)
>
> **Erin:** *I want to add to what was just said. It's how long his hair has been growing since his hair started, beginning at 24 inches.*
>
> **Chloe:** *Can I say something I noticed about the question?*
>
> **Holly:** *Yeah.*

Chloe: *I noticed that the rate was in months, but the question just says a year.*

Holly: *That's a great observation.*

Erin: *I noticed that the question is about how long his hair will be, so the answer will be in inches instead of months.*

Holly and Ellie then asked the class to solve for how long his hair would be in one year.

They also asked the class to think about how long his hair would be in the intermediate months (after one month, two months, three months) to consider the recursive relationship—adding one-half inch each month—and comparing the different ways of calculating the total if we know the number of months (Figures 3.10 and 3.11).

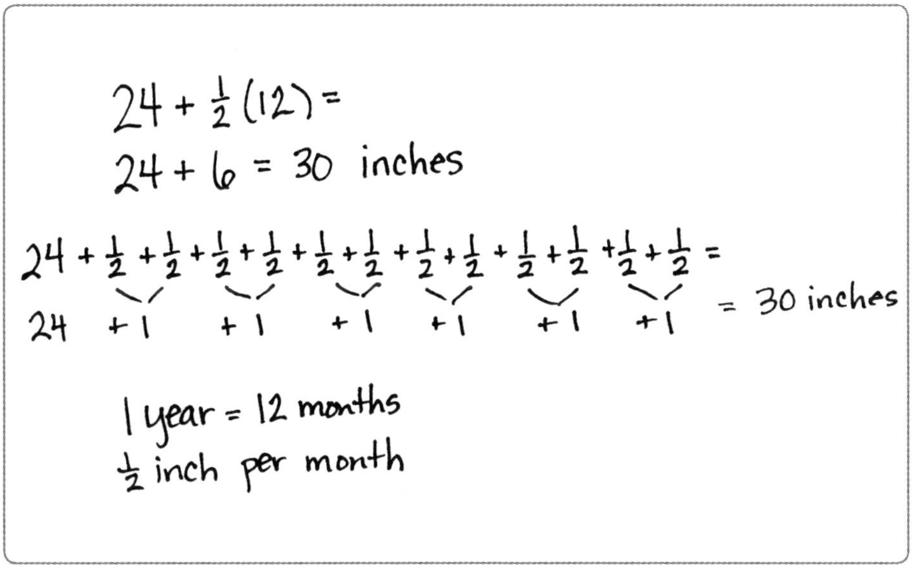

Figure 3.10
One way of showing the growth of a half-inch per month over twelve months

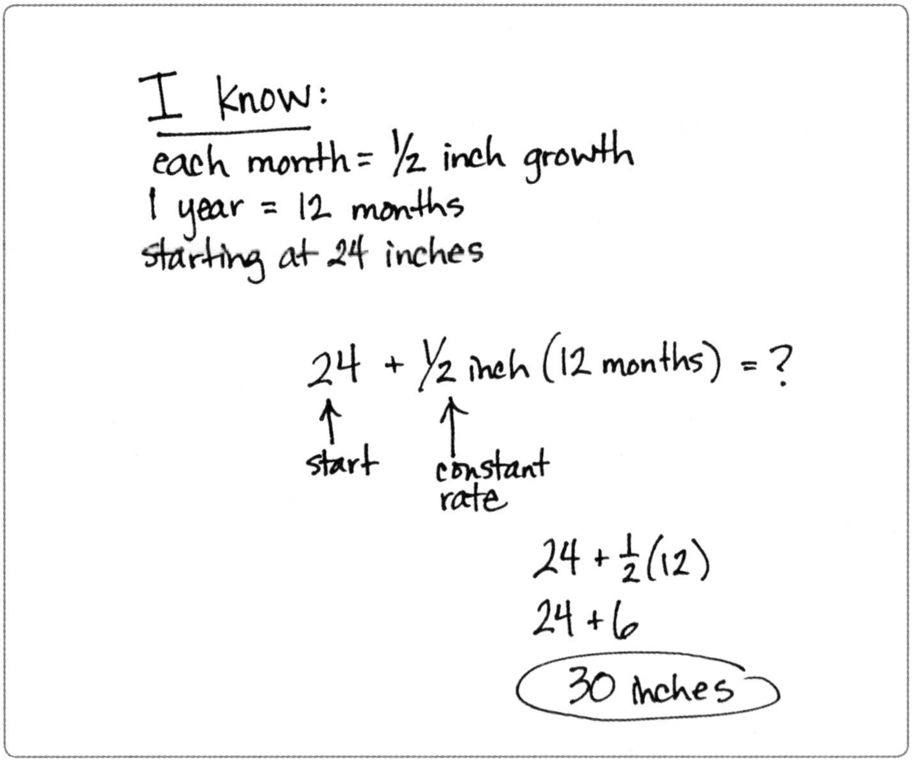

Figure 3.11
Another way of showing the growth of a half-inch per month over twelve months

In addition, they asked students to represent the data in both a table and a coordinate graph. The learning goal of the problem was to generate a range of ways to conceptualize relationships between independent and dependent variables. Before they asked their students to think about the relationship as coordinating quantities that vary, they wanted their students to think about various ways of calculating and representing a particular instance in the relationship

A story problem task that leaves out the question, requiring students to think about the structure of a story problem, supports students with making sense of the task. Without the question, students do not quickly start calculating answers. Instead, they can think about the structure of the task, consider the relationships between quantities, and generate possible questions themselves. When students experience Bet Lines, they are asked to predict about the problem, including possible questions they could ask about the situation.

Teachers can use a variety of approaches to engage learners in rough draft thinking around conceptualizing a task other than Bet Lines. A common alternative approach is a Three Reads launch (Kelemanik et al. 2016), such that students read through a story problem three times. With the first read-through, students could consider what is generally happening in the context of the problem. During the next read, they could think about what the question is asking. In the third read, students could reflect on what quantities or other information in the problem is relevant and important. The larger notion here is that when we implement tasks, students' talk about how they're making sense of the problem itself is a part of working on understanding.

Inspirations for Tasks, Not Prescriptions

To support rough draft thinking while launching a task, teachers can give students a chance to conceptualize the mathematics task through exploratory talk. The key is to scaffold discussion around the task in a way that does not reduce the cognitive demand. Instead, discussion can be structured so students think more deeply about what's happening in the problem, its structure, and the goal of the problem. Scaffolding entry into a mathematical task does not need to look like modeling how to solve it or simplifying the problem to reduce ambiguity. Rather, scaffolding can look like negotiating meaning around the task (Anghileri 2006). Discussing the task to better conceptualize it involves rough draft thinking because students are engaging in exploratory talk and working on their understanding of the problem itself, revising their thinking about the problem. Bet Lines, Three Reads, and Notice and Wonder are launching routines that provide this kind of support.

I hope that the task features and implementation ideas in this chapter are a source of inspiration rather than a prescription. As you read through the chapter, additional types of tasks, routines, and instructional practices may have come to mind. For instance, Estimation 180 tasks (Stadel 2012) give students chances to make predictions and then revise them. When students attempt Open Middle® problems (Kaplinsky 2020), they record their initial attempts, reflect on what they learn from that attempt, and try again. Many types of tasks and approaches to implementing them can elicit students' thinking about their ideas and invite students to revisit their thinking. But if students are only asked to calculate by following prescribed steps in math class, then they will not have chances to communicate to develop their understanding.

Providing space and time for students to engage in revising is at the heart of rough draft math. This process is supported by tasks that invite students to work on their understandings and teachers' instructional practices that invite revising. In Chapter 4, we will explore ways that teachers explicitly incorporate revision into math classrooms.

CHAPTER FOUR

REFINING UNDERSTANDING THROUGH REVISING IN MATH CLASS

> I see some adjustments happening. That's exactly why we share out. If you need to add on or change your responses, do so at this time.
>
> —Ms. Katrina Lindo, William Penn High School, New Castle, Delaware

Katrina Lindo started her ninth-grade class with a warm-up problem, followed by a discussion. The purpose of sharing out was for students to continue learning, so Katrina asked students to revise their individual work after the whole-class discussion. When she gave students directions about revision, not only did Katrina ask students who were incorrect to fix their answers; rather, she asked all students to adjust and add on to their work. This distinction matters because even correct work can be improved. According to Katrina, "It is important for students to value thinking and ideas of their peers, because together we can make much more progress." Katrina provides regular opportunities for students to revise their work in response to alternative viewpoints.

We don't want students' ideas to remain rough. Engaging students in rough draft thinking includes helping students revise to move toward progressively less rough thinking. The purpose of this chapter is to explore explicit revision structures, or instructional moves that create time and space for students to revise their thinking. During these revision structures, students organize and document changes in their thinking. Revision structures elicit students' thinking, elicit their awareness of how their thinking shifted, and invite students to record these shifts in their thinking. Table 4.1 lists some possibilities for revision structures for different purposes. These are not the only pedagogical structures for revising thinking during math lessons, and I hope they provide inspiration for additional options. We'll explore each in turn.

REVISION STRUCTURES

Purpose of Revision Structures	Examples of Revision Structures
Revise Solutions: Elicit, explore, and improve work on a solution for a task.	• Revise the Warm-Up • My Favorite Rough Draft • Round of Rough Draft Sharing
Revise Ideas: Elicit, explore, and improve expressions of thinking about what might be true. Explore a conjecture or potentially true statement.	• Create, Justify, or Refute a Claim • Talking Points
Reflect on Revisions: Record changes in thinking and notice how thinking has shifted.	• I used to think. . . . Now I think . . . • Stronger and Clearer Each Time, documented with a Rough Draft Thinking Revision Protocol

TABLE 4.1

Revise Solutions

One purpose for revising in math class is to work on improving solutions to mathematical tasks. An improvement might be to correct an incorrect solution, but it could also be to choose a different strategy to use or refine work with a particular strategy. In all of these structures, (1) teachers elicit students' initial thinking, (2) students explore and think about their thinking or perhaps peers' thinking, and (3) students improve their work or their peers' work.

Revise Solutions: Revise the Warm-Up

Revise the Warm-Up is a structure that can be used for students to revise individual work on a math task. Eli Tinkelman, a fifth-grade teacher at Hollin Meadows Elementary in Fairfax County, Virginia, uses a Revise the Warm-Up structure:

REVISE THE WARM-UP

- Launch a challenging but accessible task at the beginning of a math lesson.
- Ask students to write a draft of their initial thinking about this task.
- Conduct the lesson: give students learning experiences that can impact their thinking on that task.
- Revisit and revise the original task: At the end of the lesson, ask students to revise their initial thinking on the task using a different writing instrument (e.g., a pen instead of a pencil).

For this revision structure, Eli starts mathematics lessons with a relatively accessible, but still challenging math problem—a problem that students have enough prior knowledge to begin solving. He then teaches a lesson that gives students learning experiences designed to nudge their thinking about the content in the warm-up. After the lesson, Eli has students revise their work on the earlier warm-up problem using a different writing implement. If they wrote original work in pencil, their revision could be in marker or pen. This process allows students to see how their thinking evolved from the beginning of the lesson *and* gives Eli access to students' learning from that lesson. According to Eli, this feels like giving students an "exit ticket" problem at the beginning of the lesson and then giving students opportunities to revise it at the end of the lesson. Let's look at an example of how this lesson structure unfolds in his classroom.

Prior to this lesson, Eli had been working with his students on equality. He wanted students to think about visual diagrams that represented equality and unknowns, so he asked them to interpret the visual diagram shown in Figure 4.1 at both the beginning and the end of his lesson. He wanted students to interpret the diagram prior to receiving instruction about how to interpret the model, and he hoped they would draw on their prior experiences from Number Talks about equality.

At the beginning of the lesson, Eli gave his students the diagram and

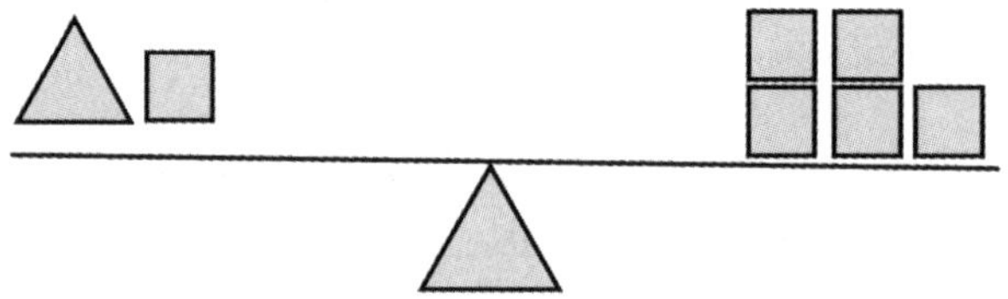

Figure 4.1
Diagram in Eli's warm-up

told them that each square represented the number one, and the triangle on the left side of the balance bar represented an unknown value, *n*. He asked them, in written prompts: *How does this picture relate to math? Could you write an equation that matches the picture? What thoughts do you have about n, or the unknown value, in this picture?* Students wrote their first thoughts in marker and then revised them at the end of the lesson in pencil.

At the beginning of the lesson, Jimmy wrote, *n is in the tenths place, so 21 + 5*. This student's thinking is so revealing! For instance, Jimmy made an assumption that instead of adding two quantities represented by shapes (triangle plus square), each shape represented a digit. It made me wonder how Jimmy thought about place value more broadly: Is the 2 in 21 representing 2 tens or 20 ones or just the number 2? Otherwise, this is an interesting notion, that the triangle and the square are two digits. (Why does the triangle represent twenty and not, say, thirty or forty?) Second, Jimmy's use of "+" is striking. He did not seem to assume that the balance beam represented equality. Combining all of the items on the balance beam in terms of addition seems like a plausible option as well. So, one thing Eli learned from eliciting initial drafts from his students is that the balance bar or teeter-totter metaphor did not necessarily convey equality, unless he helped his students see that it could.

During the lesson, the class worked in small groups on true/false equations (such as $7 + 2 = 9 + 1$ to recognize that this is false and explain why). Eli then introduced the students to an unknown, first with a blank spot ($7 + \_\_ = 9$) and then with an "n" ($6 + n = 9$). At that point, he introduced a visual diagram to students that was similar to the warm-up problem.

When they revisited this problem at the end of the lesson, Jimmy revised $21 + 5$ to $n1 = 5$. Although this is not quite where Eli wanted him to land in his thinking, Eli focused on how the representation now illustrated equality for Jimmy. The goal of the task was not only to find the value of the unknown triangle but also to develop a stronger understanding of the concept of equality as it is represented in a balance bar diagram, which is a different goal than determining the value represented by the triangle. Rather than focus on what was lacking in the student's thinking, Eli was pleased to recognize how Jimmy's thinking had evolved. Eli was oriented to notice positive growth in his student's thinking.

Another student, Anya, initially wrote, *Maybe it's like* ___ + ___ = ___. At the end of the lesson, she wrote, *It's 4 + 1 so that equils 5.* When asked whether she could write an equation that matched the picture, she initially wrote, *It could be any number, so no.* At the end of the lesson, Anya wrote, *n could be any number, so it's 4.* For her thoughts about n in the picture, she wrote at first, *It is confusing.* By the end of the lesson, Anya wrote, *It makes sence now because you have to figure out what n is.* One evolution in Anya's thinking is that, at the end of the lesson, she could articulate what the diagram represented in terms of quantities ($4 + 1 = 5$), whereas prior to the lesson, she had an idea that it was something plus something equals something. At the beginning of the lesson, she thought she could not write an equation because n could be anything, but at the end of the lesson, she realized she could put n into the equation to represent "4," "because you have to figure out what *n* is." Anya went from feeling confused to gaining some clarity.

Eli had been trying this lesson structure—having students write down their initial thinking on a task before the lesson and then having them revise their thinking on that task after the lesson (or doing the exit ticket before and after the lesson)—for a couple of weeks at this point. One reflection from Eli was that he was "realizing that the more open-ended the exit task, the more interesting revision we will see." This is true for any effort to support rough draft thinking. If the task is open enough to elicit a range of interpretations, then students will have a number of ways to connect with the task and potentially revise their understandings.

As he reflected on his use of Revise the Warm-Up, Eli wrote:

> I think this [opportunity to revise their thinking] helped kids reflect on the lesson: It's not about just *Do you know how to do this?* at the end of the lesson, but it helps kids see how their new understanding is different from the old one.

—Eli Tinkelman, elementary math teacher

Revise Solutions: My Favorite Rough Draft

Stefanie Vascellaro, a sixth-grade teacher at Meredith Middle School in the Appoquinimink School District in Middletown, Delaware, created an instructional routine that she called My Favorite Rough Draft.

First, Stefanie's students work in pairs to write a rough draft of an explanation. While students are working, Stefanie circulates and considers which explanations might be fruitful to revise together. She selects one based on her mathematical and social goals for the class and then pulls the large group together to discuss it. She displays it anonymously, and the class works together to improve the explanation. She modified this routine from *My Favorite No* (Teaching Channel 2011), which is when a teacher chooses a common procedural error and discusses with the class what was correct about the work and where it needed to be improved. Stefanie has her students write explanations for why procedural mistakes were errors rather than explaining the error to her students herself.

MY FAVORITE ROUGH DRAFT

- Launch a task that involves writing an explanation, an argument, or a justification.
- Students have individual thinking time to work on the task.
- Students discuss the task in pairs.
- Pairs of students collaboratively write a first draft of their explanation, argument, or justification.
- Two pairs of students join to make a group of four, and they trade and read peers' first drafts.
- Peers provide feedback.
- Pairs revise their first drafts.
- While students work, the teacher circulates around room to purposefully select a draft for the class to revise together.
- The teacher displays the draft (potentially anonymously) on a document camera.
- Students improve the draft by identifying its strengths and opportunities for improvement.

As an example, she asked pairs of students to write about the following:

Read and answer the problem with your shoulder partner. Explain whether the expression on the left side of the equal sign is equivalent to the expression on the right side. Show all work.

$$14x^2 + 6 - 9x^2 + 4x = 9x^2 + 6$$

She assumed that students would combine $14x^2$ and $-9x^2$ with $4x$ rather than recognize that $4x$ was a term that could not be combined with the other two terms. One of the goals for this task was for students to go beyond catching an error to interpreting why someone might do this. Students were expected to reflect on the meaning of "combining like terms." Stefanie also wanted students to practice using language of the discipline of mathematics, such as *combine like terms*, *coefficient*, *constant*, *variable*, *expression*, and *exponent*.

During My Favorite Rough Draft, students' thinking is first elicited when they talk through their initial explanations—before they write. When sixth grader Arturo talked through his ideas for his explanation with his partner, his rough draft thinking sounded like this:

> **Arturo:** *But then you have to think about it. You can't do an exponent if you're using—so, it's* 5x *to the second power* (after combing $14x^2$ with $-9x^2$)*. You can't do* 5x *to the second power plus* 4x*. It doesn't work. Because* 4x*, it would have to go to the second power. You can't add a second power to that.*

You can hear the initial roughness in Arturo's thinking when he cuts himself off ("if you're using—"). Also, the repetitiveness in his talk is what often happens when we're sorting out our thoughts.

After each pair talked and then wrote a draft, Stefanie had two pairs of students join to make groups of four, which is a structure she used frequently so students gain additional perspectives. The pairs swapped their drafts and edited one another's work by suggesting revisions to their peers' drafts. After a few minutes of editing, they got to see revisions from their peers.

When Stefanie circulated the class to choose her Favorite Rough Draft, many of the drafts were correct, so Stefanie chose a draft to revise with the class that could have included more mathematical terms. For instance, Stefanie wanted students to use terminology such as *exponents*. We can see in the students' rough draft talk that they did not use that term.

COMPARING AND CONTRASTING REVISION STRUCTURES

My Favorite No Error Analysis	***My Favorite Rough Draft*** Explanation Analysis
Display a student's (anonymous) solution.	Display a student's (anonymous) explanation—one that could use improvement (more precise, more illuminating, more concise, etc.).
Discuss what is correct about the procedures used and where and why the error took place.	Discuss what is effective about the explanation and how it could be improved and why.
Position the error as common (something multiple people might do) and helpful to learn from.	Position the explanation as helpful to learn from.

TABLE 4.2

Choosing a draft to revise as a class involves choosing student work that needs improving in a particular way for a particular reason. Perhaps we want students' revisions to include more visual illustrations, to use precise vocabulary, to make their points more clearly, or to make connections more explicit. But when looking for a Favorite Rough Draft, whether or not it is correct, it is useful to look for the strengths in that draft so the class can build on them. In other words, even as we select a goal for improvement, we should also notice and highlight the productive thinking in the original draft, which helps us all learn what to do similarly next time. Critique involves recognizing what is working as well as improving what is not working.

While revising the draft, Stefanie asked students to recommend changes and to give justifications for those suggestions. Not all changes are improvements! Suggestions for changes are stronger when the people making the suggestions justify why the change makes the draft stronger. In addition to revealing students' mathematical thinking, hearing students' justifications also provides insight as to whether students are attending to the goal for revision. Revising work as a class helps students learn to accept feedback as well.

To validate students' thinking, Stefanie explained how revising the draft supported the group's learning. She said that she displayed the students' draft anonymously to protect students who may otherwise feel uncomfortable having their work critiqued by peers. A second benefit is that an anonymous draft can help the revision process feel collectively owned by the group: the draft becomes the class's draft, and the entire class benefits from the opportunity to think it through. If we make this explicit—the ways in which the draft helps everyone's thinking improve—then the author of the draft is positioned as having contributed something valuable to the class.

Consider phasing out the use of anonymous drafts. After norms are in place such that in-progress thinking is seen as valuable, students can feel safer having their work publicly revised with their name attached to it. If we highlight strengths in the draft while revising, students might even feel proud of their drafts.

My Favorite Rough Draft involves multiple cycles of revision. After thinking individually, students share that initial thinking with their partners. Through cocreating a written draft with a peer, their own ideas might shift. Pairs of students then trade with another pair of students and receive feedback on their drafts that they can apply toward another revision. A further opportunity to revise thinking occurs when the class revises the Favorite Rough Draft selected by the teacher. In this particular example, Stefanie used this revision structure to analyze students' explanations of a procedural mistake, but you could use My Favorite Rough Draft to analyze drafts of proofs, justifications, or other forms of mathematical reasoning.

Revise Solutions: Rounds of Rough Draft Sharing

The third example of a revision structure for revising solutions to problems was described in Chapter 2 in Brandy Cooper's Rounds of Rough Draft Sharing. When students work in groups, Brandy asks students to create rough draft solutions. She stops group work before the groups completely finish the problem and has the class share out their rough drafts. She makes it clear that students should seek to understand one another's work rather than critique it. Then, after each Round of Rough Draft Sharing, groups go back and continue to work on the problem, incorporating what they'd learned from the sharing out of rough drafts into their revisions.

A key element in Brandy's Rounds of Rough Draft Sharing was asking students to talk about their drafts publicly before students felt their work was finished. Before implementing this revision structure, Brandy's students had performed to one another rather than learning from one another if all

ROUNDS OF ROUGH DRAFT SHARING

- Launch a low-floor/high-ceiling, open-ended task.
- In small groups, students work on a rough draft solution.
- Round of rough draft sharing: regroup as a class before small groups have reached resolution on their thinking—students share their group drafts.
- During rough draft sharing, peers seek to understand rather than critique (nonevaluative stance).
- After rough draft sharing, groups return to their solutions to revise their thinking.
- Groups then share their revised drafts.
- Repeat as needed.

or most students had completed their work prior to sharing out. Previously, students were also less driven to listen to understand peers' solutions when they were already sure about their own solutions. However, during Rounds of Rough Draft Sharing, they shared before they felt done with their work, so students were more engaged and open to feedback.

Another important part of rough draft sharing in Brandy's classroom was to ask students to provide nonevaluative feedback to one another. Students needed to understand their peers' work before giving advice to improve it. Sentence starters helped students learn to interact with one other's thinking: "I wonder why you . . ." or "Tell me more why you . . ."

A more detailed description of Rounds of Rough Draft Sharing can be found in Chapter 2.

Revise Ideas

Students can do more than solve problems in a math class: students can also consider what is true. They can make generalizations or claims about what seems to be true and then explore and improve their expressions through revision. These revision structures give students opportunities to revise their thinking about concepts and conjectures.

Revise Ideas: Create, Justify, or Refute a Claim

Molly Brnich, a seventh-grade teacher at Meredith Middle School in the Appoquinimink School District in Middletown, Delaware, asks her students to make claims in the form of conjectures about what they think is true and then make arguments that justify or refute those claims. In the beginning of the year, Molly tells students that mathematicians notice and generalize patterns, so they can expect to spend class time noticing patterns and making general claims because they are mathematicians as well. This revision structure is called Create, Justify, or Refute a Claim.

CREATE, JUSTIFY, OR REFUTE A CLAIM

- Structure an exploration for students aligned with goals for their learning.
- Students generate claims about what might be true by noticing and wondering as they explore.
- Make a public record of a list of student-generated claims about the phenomenon being explored.
- Students research claims, either seeking counter-examples that refute the claim or justifying that the claim is true.

Molly regularly gave students a full class period to explore using manipulatives or data sets and then asked them to record patterns and relationships they noticed or wondered about while they worked. For instance, Molly's students used Polystrips to generate claims related to relationships between side lengths of triangles. She wanted them to observe the triangle inequality such that the third side of a triangle is shorter than the other two sides added together. One way that they could see this would be through trying to construct triangles and observing combinations of side lengths that did not make a triangle (Figure 4.2).

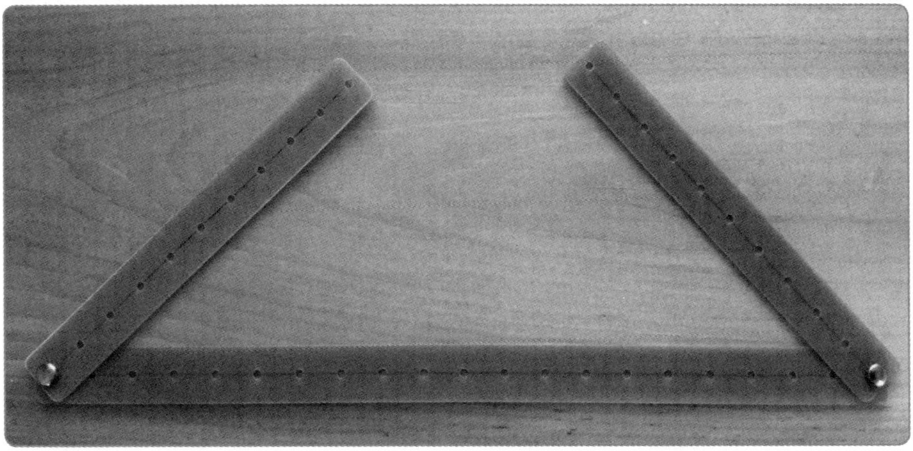

Figure 4.2
Polystrips with side lengths of ten, twenty, and ten that do not make a triangle

In Molly's class, students learn to make conjectures through observing what they notice and stating what they think is happening. When they noticed a pattern, Molly would ask the students to make a related claim. For instance, "Ms. B, all of the angles in a triangle are adding up to 180 degrees." Molly would reply, "Is there something you would like to say is always true based on that?" The student: "I think all of the angles in a triangle add up to 180 degrees." Molly encouraged the student: "Okay. That's a claim you are making." Molly initially identified claims like this as students made them. Students eventually shifted to asserting that they had a claim without her prompting, and they would move right to writing it on the whiteboard.

Students had to learn how to purposefully explore. Early in the school year, students played more than they purposefully explored. Molly was comfortable with some amount of playing as a part of exploring; it is useful to play with new tools to see how they operate. But she ultimately wanted to help students "play with purpose." Molly would remind students of the purpose of finding patterns and relationships as they played. If Molly saw a student's work devolving to the point where their play no longer seemed to hold a purpose, she would ask the student to pick a claim that had been written on the board and ask the student to research or explore that claim.

Once enough claims were generated, Molly selected claims for the class to examine that related to her goals for their learning. She invited the class to investigate whether the claims were true or to come up with counterexamples to refute them.

> They [students] either need to find if that works every time, and, if it does, then why? We talk about how math makes sense. There's got to be a reason to make sense of that. Or they could find a counterexample and disprove it. Generally, we start by: *What do you notice or wonder here?* As they work, they'll look at their claims as they're exploring. Sometimes they'll pick a claim to try to explore and see if it's true. Or they find that a claim is not true, and they go to the board and draw a little arrow, and write, *I disagree because . . .* or *I agree with this part because of this*.
>
> —Molly Brnich, middle school math teacher

Students are empowered as authorities for deciding what is true about mathematics in Molly's classroom.

For a different exploration, Molly asked her students to compare the length across a circle (diameter) with the length of the distance around a circle (circumference). Using string and rulers, students measured a number of circular and cylindrical objects. Students were invited to write claims about what they thought could be happening. What relationships or patterns did they notice and wonder about?

During this exploration, her students wrote these ideas on the board:

- *Is the circumference double the diameter?*
- *Maybe the diameter is 3 to 4 times smaller than circumference.*

The class decided then to explore whether any of these ideas were true. The students did more measuring and comparing. A student refined the original claims to *Diameter x 3ish = Circumference*. Another student wondered, *Are all circles scaled copies of other circles, if the diameter is always three-ish times smaller (than the circumference)?* The students continued to revise their thinking about the relationship between circumference and diameter through more measurements.

Molly developed these units in collaboration with another seventh-grade teacher, Nicole Crawford, at nearby Redding Middle School in the same school district. They frequently shared their students' claims with each other. For example, in another unit, Molly sent one of her students' claims about similar figures to Nicole for Nicole's class to investigate: *If you add the same amount to every side, you would have a similar figure*. Nicole's students researched the claim, and each table group created a PowerPoint slide refuting it.

For example, some students in Nicole's class wrote, *We want to disprove Ms. Brnich's class, because we think that you don't need to add the same amount to each side to get a similar figure*. Students provided specific counterexamples and diagrams to refute the claim, such as one student who created a diagram of two similar triangles and wrote, *As you can see, I added 2 units to each side length. Then the angle measure turned out different. A similar figure has the same angle measures. Therefore, this does not work to make a similar figure*. Another student wondered, *Would this claim work for squares since at least all squares already have all the same side lengths?* A student in Molly's class responded, *So from this I can see when increasing, you must use the same ratio*. In these ways, Molly's and Nicole's students engaged in mathematical argumentation.

Students in Molly's classes developed a sense of pride around generating claims.

I just love it because they're talking about other people, their thinking, and it's just empowering those kids. I have one girl who asked me not to erase her claim yet. This is a girl who said that she hated math. She made one claim that we proved true: *If you add a number and its opposite, you'll always get zero*. Now people in class will say, "I made zero pairs when I added, because Marlene said when you add the opposite, you get zero." We proved that to be true. Once they've proved it, they can use that claim in their reasoning. It's really cool. I see Marlene have a smile on her face when someone talks about her claim. Sometimes kids are like, my claim was way wrong, but at least I got you guys to think about it!

—Molly Brnich

Molly strives to help her students develop their authority around mathematical argumentation and reasoning. One of Molly's students said,

> *I get to hear about what other people think and use it in my reasoning. I also like when we get feedback on our own claims because everything in math comes from our own ideas, and Ms. B's not telling us rules. The rules are what we create.*

Another student said,

> *I guess it's better to be sure because I understand it than to be sure because a teacher told me, so I'll just keep asking questions until it makes sense to me.*

Molly shared that her students debated for quite a while about whether 4 inches, 4 inches, and 8 inches made a triangle, and when someone said, "Another teacher told me that it doesn't so this group is right," a student replied, "I think it's my right to be convinced and to not believe you until I understand why." Molly wants the process of making and investigating claims to empower her students.

If they're wondering something, it's often something I'm trying to get at in my lesson, so let's explore that. It's now Ralph's wonderment that we're exploring, not Ms. B's "essential question," you know? Sometimes they don't come up with anything that we're exploring but getting them to just stop and notice. I think it helps with their problem solving. They don't even know what they're looking for, but they are just

> noticing different things about it. So, if I give them a problem they don't know how to solve, they're automatically starting to think, okay, what do I notice? Maybe that can help.
>
> —Molly Brnich

Students even started to make claims on their own at home. While working on subtracting integers at home, a student wrote this claim on a whiteboard, took a picture, and sent it to Molly: *If the first number is positive and the second is negative, the answer will always be positive.* Molly was delighted to put the claim on the board during the integers unit so the class could explore it.

Molly asked her students to reflect on their experience in her classroom regularly. Once when she asked her students about the most important thing they learned in her class so far, a student wrote, *The most important thing I learned so far is that I have the right to be confused. That really helped me because I always thought being confused was bad.* Creating, justifying, and refuting claims creates a learning environment where confusion is a typical experience, because everyone is trying to decide whether a relationship or pattern exists. No one knows for sure yet. Molly asked her students what they are most proud of about their class, and a student wrote, *I like how we can share our unfinished thinking without worrying if it's wrong.* Molly treats all students' claims as worthy of consideration, and she creates space for students to explore their claims and one another's claims.

The spirit of rough drafting is constantly taking place when teachers like Molly and Nicole use the structure of Create, Justify, or Refute a Claim.

Revise Ideas: Talking Points Protocol

Kathleen Wilson, a high school teacher at St. Georges Technical High School in Middletown, Delaware, uses a Talking Points protocol as a revision structure. A Talking Points protocol gives students a chance to express their rough draft ideas about whether a statement (or a *talking point*) is true. Students also listen to others' rough draft ideas and then revise their thinking. This process happens in small groups (Dawes 2012; Statmore 2014).

The Talking Points protocol starts with teacher-created statements about mathematics that may or may not be true or may be partially true. Students discuss each statement in three rounds. During the first round, the group considers the statement, and each person states whether they agree, disagree, or are unsure about that statement. Importantly, each person also provides a reason to justify why they think the statement is or is not true. Everyone in the group shares in turn in a round-robin structure with no discussion.

For the second round, after listening to what others have said, each person then takes a turn (again in a round-robin approach without discussion), and states whether they agree, disagree, or are unsure about the statement, justifying their position. After having heard from group members,

TALKING POINTS PROTOCOL

- The teacher generates a list of talking points—statements that are true, partially true, or false—and gives the list of talking points to students in small groups.
- Round 1: The students in the group each state whether they agree, disagree, or are unsure. They give their reasons why. Everyone goes in turn with no discussion or cross talk.
- Round 2: After listening to their peers, students go around again and state whether they agree, disagree, or are unsure about that statement. They are likely to have been influenced by some of what they heard from their peers in their reasons why, even if their initial stance toward the statement did not change.
- Round 3: The group tallies their opinions about the statement.
- Repeat these three rounds for each talking point.

students will likely have revised their position about the statement, revised their justification for the position, or both.

Then, for the third round, the group tallies the final opinions: the number of people who agree with the statement, the number of people who disagree, and the number of people who remain unsure. At this point, the group moves on to the next statement. A key aspect of a Talking Points protocol is that students are not voicing whether they agree or disagree with one another. Rather, they are explaining the extent to which they agree or disagree with the statement about mathematics.

Kathleen Wilson gave her students these talking points to consider:

KATHLEEN WILSON'S TALKING POINTS

1. **Since $\sqrt{a}\sqrt{b} = \sqrt{ab}$, then $\sqrt{-5}\sqrt{-5} = \sqrt{25} = 5$.**
2. **All cubic functions have at least one real solution.**
3. **Only quadratic functions can have complex solutions.**
4. **Operations with complex numbers (such as +, −, ×, ÷) can have solutions that are real.**

Through discussing these four statements, students could push their own thinking about real numbers, irrational numbers, and complex numbers. Because students were expected to justify why the statement is or is not true or the ways in which it is not quite true, they had to think about ideas and concepts and go beyond describing procedures to do so.

For Round 1, when they shared their thinking about the first statement, a group of students talked about whether they agreed, disagreed, or were unsure.

> **Colt:** *Well, I disagree because you can't take a square root of a negative number.*
>
> **Fatima:** *I'm unsure, because I don't know what to do about the order of operations here. Are we multiplying or are we square-rooting?*

Titus: *I am unsure, too, because I don't really know what's going on.*

Camille: *I also said I was unsure, because, you know, we just did imaginary numbers. If you took the imaginary number and did 5 and negative 1, it would just be 5*i*. I mean, is it going to multiply to be 25? I really don't know.*

Fatima: *I'm thinking. So, if it was, it'd be 5*i *times 5*i*, which would be 25*i*-squared, which would be negative 25.*

Camille: *Which still wouldn't be 25.*

Fatima: *It'd be 5.*

Camille: *I feel like this is missing an* i*. It'd still have to have an* i*, if it was going to be negative. That makes sense, kind of.*

Titus: *I agree.*

Camille: *I just feel like because this is positive, these aren't the same. I'm still kind of unsure.*

Colt: *Like I said, I disagree, because if you were to factor that out, you'd get the square root of 5 and the square root of negative 1, which is—*

Camille: *Yeah, that's what I was—*

Colt: *—square root of 5*i*, and as he said, square root of 5*i *times the square root of 5*i *would be* (pause)*—not that.*

Camille (laughs): *Yeah, that's what I was saying when I was explaining why I was unsure, because if you do 5*i *and 5*i*, I just feel like you're not going to get 5 even, regardless of what you do.*

The protocol gave most students in this group a voice to talk about their ideas and share when their thinking shifted after hearing from one another (although we did not hear much from Titus). Colt and Fatima were able to articulate their mathematical thinking more strongly after hearing from Camille, but they did so in their own words. Students also became more certain about their justifications. During Round 2, when students went around again, fewer students were unsure about their stance toward the statement after hearing from their peers.

During a structured Talking Points protocol, students can revise their thinking at least two times. This protocol is especially useful to teach students careful listening to support revision.

Reflect on Revisions

Another purpose of a revision structure is to help students become aware of changes in their thinking. Students can reflect on how their thinking has changed, document changes in their thinking, and consider what inspired the changes in their thinking. When we ask students to reflect on how their thinking has shifted, they engage in a metacognitive process.

In contrast, for the other types of revision structures, explicitly generating ideas and revising them tends to go something like this:

GENERAL PROCESS FOR REVISING SOLUTIONS OR IDEAS

1. **Get thinking out—about solutions or ideas. (Brainstorm. Freewrite.)**
2. **Look back and reflect on the initial thinking. Make these initial ways of thinking an object of reflection.**
3. **Recognize where there is potential to extend, to refine, or to change one's thinking. Identify changes that can be made.**
4. **Make those changes.**
5. **Repeat.**

However, sometimes our thinking changes so subtly that we might not notice the shifts at first. If we pause, stop, and think about our thinking, only then might we realize that we used to think one way and now we think differently.

Reflect on Revisions: I Used to Think . . . But Now I Think . . .

One of my favorite moves to explicitly incorporate revision into teaching is to use the sentence starter: "I used to think. . . . But now, I think . . ." This is a useful approach for making students' thinking visible to themselves and others (Harvard Graduate School of Education 2011).

I USED TO THINK . . . BUT NOW I THINK . . .

- **Reserve about five minutes at the end of a lesson or activity for an exit ticket.**
- **Distribute a note card or half sheet of paper to every student.**
- **Give students time to reflect individually about how their thinking changed during the lesson or activity.**
- **Each student responds to the following sentence starter in writing: "I used to think. . . . But now I think ..."**
- **Collect from students.**

It takes about five minutes to ask students to reflect on changes in their thinking. This revision structure makes for a particularly good end-of-lesson closure. This time is well spent because students develop awareness of how their thinking has shifted, which helps them value their learning experiences and appreciate the growth in their thinking. They also have opportunities to engage in mathematical reasoning when articulating changes in their thinking. It is a useful formative assessment tool for teachers, too. Students' responses can serve as feedback to teachers about whether and how a lesson is achieving its goals.

While teaching a mathematics content course for prospective elementary teachers at my university, I taught some lessons on proportional relationships. One of my goals was to help prospective teachers see that they did not need to rely on the cross-multiplication procedure to solve a missing value proportion problem. I wanted to help them use alternative strategies for solving these problems, and I wanted them to see that these alternative strategies made sense conceptually.

Among other tasks, the prospective teachers worked on the following story problem:

> On a map, $\frac{1}{3}$ inch represents 10 miles. If two cities are $2\frac{1}{2}$ inches inches apart on the map, what is the distance between them in miles?

I asked the prospective teachers to solve the problem in whatever way made sense to them. In previous lessons, we had already discussed solutions using cross multiplication. I asked them to explain why those solutions made sense, and prospective teachers could not explain them. Preservice teachers were aware that they were expected only to use solutions that they could explain.

Two related solutions arose. For one solution, the student found the number of miles associated with one inch. (Thirty miles represented by one inch. Three groups of one-third of an inch to make one inch means three groups of ten miles to make thirty miles.) Then, once they knew the number of miles for one inch, they found two and a half groups of that distance to see how many miles were represented in two and a half inches, which was seventy-five miles. This was a unit rate approach. Find a unit rate, or miles per one inch, then scale up by the total number of inches to find the total number of miles.

For the second solution, a student worked with equivalent ratios and scaled up and down. She realized that one-third of an inch was also two-sixths of an inch. Then she partitioned the distance (ten miles) for one-third of an inch into two parts to find the equivalent ratio of one-sixth of an inch, representing five miles. The student wanted to find the distance associated with two and a half inches. She needed fifteen groups of one-sixth inches to get to two and a half inches, or fifteen-sixths inches. So, she found fifteen groups of five miles to get to seventy-five miles.

For both approaches, the preservice teachers represented their thinking in multiple ways. Some preservice teachers represented both the unit rate approach and the scaling up and down approach with double number lines. We solved multiple missing value proportional reasoning problems, discussed why these strategies made sense, and discussed why cross multiplication made less sense.

At the end of the second lesson of working on problems like this and discussing strategies that made sense to them, I asked my students to fill out a note card. I displayed this prompt: *Regarding solving proportional reasoning problems with cross multiplication, I used to think . . . But now I think . . .* Four of their responses follow:

- *I used to think that cross multiplication was the best strategy for solving proportions because it was the method I was taught in school, but now I think using a dual number line and scaling up and down is a better strategy because it gives you a visual and allows you to see the "why" and not just the "how."*
- *I used to think cross multiplication was the easiest way to solve proportions; however, I never really understood why it worked. I mindlessly cross multiplied to get my answer. Now I think that unit rate is the best way to solve proportions because it shows exactly how you get an answer, and you can easily see what each unit measures all the way up to the number needed to find.*
- *I used to think cross multiplying was the best way because it was fast and only took a few steps. Now I think cross multiplying is still my favorite way, but I understand how scaling shows the relationships.*
- *Regarding solving proportions with cross multiplication, I used to think it was the best method. However, now I realize that I have no clue why I cross multiply! It's just what I was taught to do. Now I think unit rate, scaling up and down, and double number lines are better methods because I am able to visualize what is going on and it makes sense.*

From my students' reflections, I read that many of them had seen relationships between quantities more clearly with the strategies that were newer to them. I read that they were, indeed, unsure how to explain cross multiplication, but some students still preferred its efficiency. I read that some students preferred a unit rate approach. Others preferred a scaling approach. Some liked both.

This quick reflection via the *I used to think. . . . But now I think . . .* prompt invited my students to become aware of and notice shifts in their thinking through writing about them, and their writing gave me valuable information about their thinking.

Reflect on Revisions: Stronger and Clearer Each Time, Documented with a Rough Draft Thinking Revision Protocol

Another approach to help students become metacognitively aware of shifts in their thinking is to provide a structure for students to notice both changes in their ideas *and* in what sparked those changes. Inspiration to revise must come from somewhere. Documenting sources of inspiration helps students keep track of the evolution of their thinking.

While working with mathematics teachers in Oregon in the Salem-Keizer Public Schools, Tom Stricklin, a high school math implementation specialist, created reflection protocols for documenting evolution in mathematical thinking. These protocols were inspired by the classroom routine of Stronger and Clearer Each Time (Zwiers et al. 2017). Stronger and Clearer Each Time is a mathematical language routine that provides an opportunity for students to revise and refine both the strength of their mathematical ideas and the clarity of their verbal and written explanations.

Stronger and Clearer Each Time is implemented through successive pair-shares. At the beginning of the routine, students write out their initial responses to a prompt. They get their ideas out in a draft form. Next, students share their initial drafts with a partner and try to share their thinking as clearly as possible so that the other person understands. The partner who listens asks clarifying questions—"Why did you think about it this way?"—to seek to understand the other student. Then, they switch roles, and the other partner explains their draft as clearly as they can and responds to the first partner's clarifying questions. When they get their papers back from their partners, in Tom's protocol, they write down paraphrased ideas of what they learned from their partner's thinking. At this point, they write a new draft. Then, they repeat the process; this time with a new partner. Finally, they go back to their initial work and revise it.

When Tom implemented this routine with students, he gave students a prompt to elicit a first draft.

> *Consider functions of the form* $\mathbf{y = mx + b}$. *What do* $\mathbf{x}$ *and* $\mathbf{y}$ *represent in this function?*
>
> *What do* $\mathbf{m}$ *and* $\mathbf{b}$ *represent? Which ones can you change?*

STRONGER AND CLEARER EACH TIME, DOCUMENTED WITH A ROUGH DRAFT THINKING REVISION PROTOCOL

- Give students a prompt to elicit a first draft.
- Individual think time: record a first draft on the protocol form.
- Trade papers with a partner. Each partner reads their peer's draft. Each person in the pair takes turns seeking to understand the other person's draft by asking clarifying questions.
- Trade papers back. Record a paraphrased version of the partner's thinking.
- Individual think time: rewrite a draft, informed by the partner's ideas.
- Trade papers with a different partner. Each partner reads their peer's draft. Each person in the pair takes turns seeking to understand the other person's draft by asking clarifying questions.
- Trade papers back. Record a paraphrased version of the partner's thinking.
- Individual think time: write a revised, final draft, informed by the second partner's ideas.

Students had private reasoning time to write out their own first drafts, recording their drafts using the protocol Tom designed (Figure 4.3).

Students wrote their rough drafts in the space on the upper left corner of the protocol. Then, after trading their papers with a partner and trying to understand each other's thinking, they took their papers back and wrote down inspiration from their partner on the right side of the page. They wrote a new draft, informed by their partner's thinking, on the left side of the page under their rough draft. With a new partner, they shared their

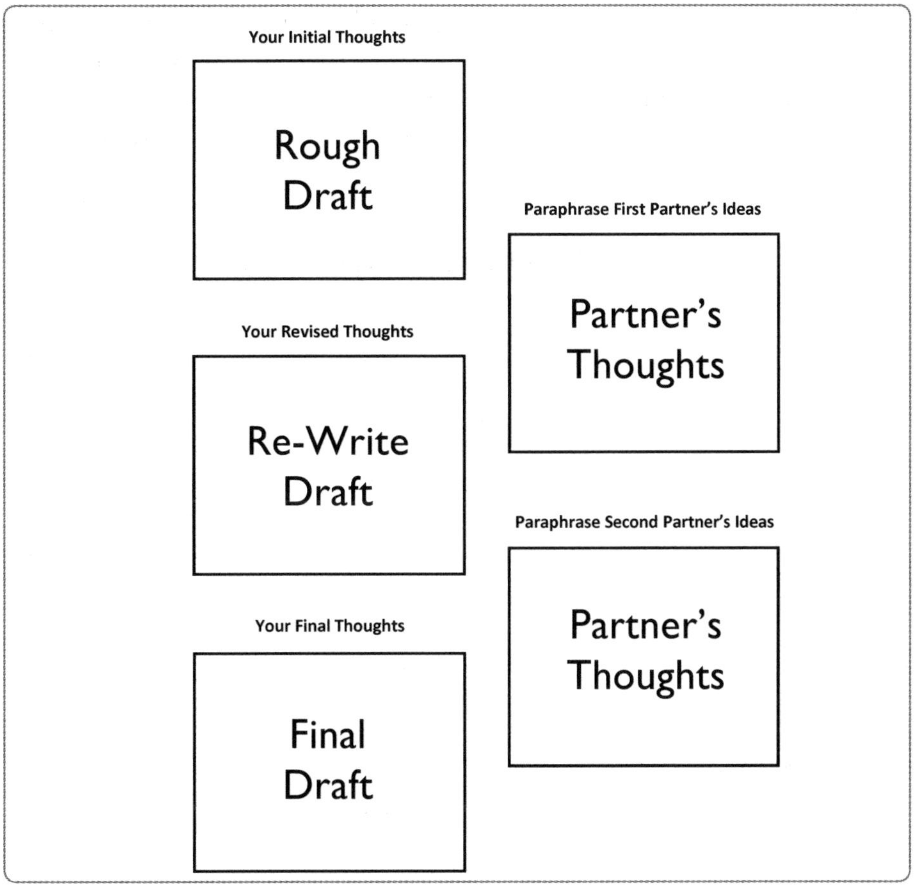

Figure 4.3
Protocol for documenting the evolution of mathematical thinking with partners

revised drafts, sought to understand each other, and recorded their partner's ideas on the left side of the page. They then wrote final drafts on the bottom of the right side of the protocol. There is power in documenting how drafts evolve and change as well as what the partner said that affected changes in drafts.

Tom also shared a related protocol that could be used to track how thinking evolved because of a whole-class discussion (Figure 4.4).

Again, with this protocol, students document what their initial ideas were on the top left side, ideas that inspire changes in their thinking on the right side, and a revision on the bottom left side. Seeing or hearing a contrasting way of thinking from a peer can be a possible source of inspiration for adjusting thinking.

This routine incorporates some powerful emphases. There is a focus on listening by seeking to understand rather than to evaluate. Hearing a partner's thinking turns into insights that support revision of one's own thinking. To revise, we need feedback. But feedback doesn't always need to

Rough Draft Processing Graphic Organizer

Initial Ideas

Ideas from Others

Revised Ideas

Figure 4.4
Documenting revisions in thinking from a whole-class discussion

look like an evaluation. Feedback could appear in the form of contrasting your own thinking with another person's explanation. The process of trying to communicate with another person can also serve as feedback. (An example of my students improving their drafts using Stronger and Clearer Each Time is described in Chapter 6.)

There is something about the nature of mathematical understanding: once we reach an understanding, it becomes so much a part of us that we forget we once lacked that understanding. Documenting shifts in our thinking normalizes the idea that changes will and should happen. Changing our minds in the face of new ideas, new information, or new perspectives is a powerful thing that smart people do all the time. Documenting the evolution of their thoughts serves students by giving them credit for growing in their understandings.

Revision Structures Can Move Along a Language Spectrum

According to Herbel-Eisenmann, Steele, and Cirillo (2013), we express ideas in the mathematics classroom in different stages of development along a language spectrum in various communication contexts. This language spectrum represents a range of ways that people communicate.

1. In small groups, students use *a language of interaction* to explore ideas together. In this exploratory phase of the language spectrum, we tend to think about rough draft talking taking place. (One relevant revision structure is Rounds of Rough Draft Sharing.)

2. During whole-class discussion, students tend to use *a language of recounting experiences*, sharing what they discussed during group-work time. However, the whole class could also jump back into a language of interaction to make sense of the ideas shared through recounting experiences and to make new connections. (A relevant revision structure is My Favorite Rough Draft.)

3. When an individual student writes out her thinking about what is true, after engaging in these phases of the language spectrum, she moves into *the language of generalizing*, or documenting what she thinks could be true by justifying why, in her own words and representations. Some of this language of generalizing may begin

to unfold in the prior communication contexts of small-group and whole-class discussions, if she is justifying a mathematical claim that she knows to be true. (One relevant revision structure is Create, Justify, or Refute Claims.)

4. Then, in contexts such as mathematics textbooks or lectures, we see the *mathematics register* phase of the language spectrum, using ways of explaining and justifying that reflect how mathematicians might present formalized ideas. (This can occur at the final stages of any revision structure.)

As we communicate to make sense of mathematics, we move through this language spectrum, often in nonlinear ways.

Herbel-Eisenmann and Cirillo (2009) describe opportunities to learn through discourse as being productive and powerful. Productive opportunities to learn give students access to mathematics content and discourse practices. Powerful opportunities to learn are ways that students can develop their identities as knowers and doers of mathematics. As we look along the language spectrum, we see productive ways that mathematical thinking grows and develops.

Why Implement Revision Structures? Mathematicians Revise

As we navigate early stages in the language spectrum—the language of interaction and the language of recounting—through an iterative, back-and-forth process, we express our best guesses. Magdalene Lampert (1990) connected back to the teacher in Lakatos's *Proofs and Refutations* (1976) who said, "I respect conscious guessing, because it comes from the best human qualities: courage and modesty" (30). The activity of doing mathematics, then, is different from recording what we have come to know. Once we know something, we express this knowledge in either the language of generalizing or the mathematics register. In the process of coming to know something, we move in nonlinear ways—zigzags—making purposeful conjectures and trying to determine whether they are true or whether we can refute them. Students benefit from hearing that nonlinear ways of making sense are normal and to be expected.

Even mathematicians who have published their proofs leave their ideas open to further investigation. The most final drafts could be reopened and considered rough drafts in the face of new ways of considering premises. According to Lampert (1990, 30), "It is this vulnerability to reexamination that allows mathematics to grow and develop." We can concurrently state our thinking with certainty and be open to have those ideas challenged further.

In her work, Lampert also directs us to George Pólya (1954) who wrote about the moral qualities required to do mathematics: intellectual courage, intellectual honesty, and wise restraint. When we are intellectually courageous, we are ready to revise something even if we believe it to be true. When we are intellectually honest, we are willing to change what we believe to be true when there is good reason to do so. But we should also exercise wise restraint in that we should not change what we believe to be true without good reason to do so and without seriously examining those reasons.

Pólya also reminds us that revision is at the heart of doing mathematics. According to Póyla, there are four steps for solving any problem: (1) understand the problem, (2) devise a strategy, (3) carry out the plan, and (4) look back on your results. After looking back on the results, mathematicians revise and repeat this process to keep pushing their thinking forward. Mathematicians revise.

Wonderments About Implementing Revision Structures

I want to acknowledge some of the complex aspects of asking students to revise their thinking during mathematics class. Doing this work with learners has raised several questions. One question is the direction or goals for revising. What students learn from revising is related to the goals we set with students for revising. I am also curious about the role of listening in a classroom where rough draft thinking and revision happen. Listening matters. Students will learn a great deal from hearing alternative perspectives, and if they are able to listen well, these alternative perspectives can provide inspiration for revising. Also, I wonder about the culture of assessment in the mathematics classroom and how it supports or undermines a culture of rough drafting. (I summarize these wonderments in Table 4.3.)

WONDERMENTS ABOUT IMPLEMENTING REVISION STRUCTURES

- Goals for Revising: What goal(s) do we set for students' revisions?
- Listening to Learn Through Revising: How do we learn to engage in pedagogical listening in ways that honor strengths in students' emerging thinking? How do we support students with learning to listen to each other by seeking to understand?
- Evaluating: How can our assessment practices align with (or not fully diverge from) our revision practices?

TABLE 4.3

Goals for Revising

When we ask students to revise their thinking, how do we want them to improve it? Setting a goal for revision can help students orient themselves amid the many ways students can refine their draft ideas.

Becoming more accurate is often how we think about revising our work in math class. Some examples of revision structures described in this chapter addressed revising for accuracy, such as My Favorite Rough Draft. However, students' definitions, proofs, justifications, or explanations could also be improved by becoming more concise, more elegant, more convincing, or even more illuminating. See Table 4.4 for several possible goals for revision.

WHY SHOULD WE REVISE OUR MATHEMATICAL THINKING?

Become More Correct	This is the most prevalent reason why we might think we need to revise our mathematical work: to correct mistakes. But this is only one reason among many to revise. Many correct solutions would benefit from additional revisions. There is more to understand about mathematics beyond seeking a correct answer.
Seek New Insights	Our initial drafts could be viewed as our first way of solving a problem or our first way of seeing a mathematical relationship. Successive drafts could include alternative solution approaches, new ways of seeing, or alternative noticings.
Become More Precise	We can examine the ways that we talk or write about mathematics to see whether we can communicate what we mean in a more exact manner. There may be more than one way to interpret an early draft, and successive revisions can help with communicating more clearly.
Become More Detailed	In our initial drafts, we may assume that audiences know what we mean. Elaborating by adding additional details to fill in where we may have made assumptions about shared understandings can improve communication.

TABLE 4.4

(continued)

Become More Concise	Early drafts often have a degree of repetition and redundancies as we talk or write to work out what makes sense to us. Some sentences might be overly wordy. Revising allows us to winnow down to the essential points.
Become More Elegant	Mathematicians often express appreciation for a proof that has beauty and elegance. The aesthetic quality of an argument can be found in its simplicity, in its transparency, in the unexpected, or in visual appeal. Perhaps we can revise our thinking and represent it in a more elegant manner.
Become More Illuminating	We can review our work by trying to switch perspectives—from speaker or writer to audience member (listener or reader)—and consider how our ideas can be represented so that they are clearer to another person. We can add examples to help the ideas come to life for the reader.
Become More Convincing	If we are trying to justify why something is true, our argument may not yet convince a skeptic. When we develop our thinking, we first convince ourselves. A next revision could convince a friend. An additional revision could convince a skeptic, which includes making sure important ideas are supported (Mason, Burton, and Stacey 2011).

TABLE 4.4

(continued)

Become More Realistic	If we are trying to write a story to represent a mathematical situation, we may first work on trying to make sure the mathematical relationships make sense. After reading the initial draft, we might realize that our situation is not realistic. A revision can address these contextual issues.
Become More Illustrative	An initial representation of our thinking might not have visual diagrams or the diagrams might not yet represent the mathematics and provide clarity to others.
Become More Connected	To see mathematics as a connected system of ideas, we could take another pass at our drafts to communicate how these ideas connect with ideas we have thought about in the past.

TABLE 4.4

How shall we choose? We could ask students to set their own goals for their revisions, to review their own writing and decide how it could be improved. They could compare and contrast their writing with a peer's writing as a way to notice alternative ways to represent their thinking. Or we might select a goal for students to emphasize from Table 4.4 that we want students to work on.

Initially, students might not be excited about an opportunity to revise because they might think of revising as fixing something that is wrong. If we think this way, revising could be one more piece of evidence that our thinking is not good enough—that we might not be good enough. Alternatively, we can think about revising as continuing to improve ideas that we already appreciate or may even love. We can recognize strengths in our thinking and see opportunities to refine and extend it.

Teachers and students benefit from talking together about the purposes of revising thinking in math class. We can take a great idea, a good beginning, some initial interesting thoughts, and make it even better. Developing a shared understanding that revising is not always repairing something that is broken can support students' engagement in revision and confidence in themselves while revising.

When I work on my own writing, my early drafts are for me. I use my writing process to sort out my thinking. I make my own ideas explicit to me by getting them out of my head. The organization of initial drafts usually looks quite different from the more final drafts. I tell myself that I have to write or talk things through just to know what I think. First drafts are for ourselves. They help us clarify our thinking and make sense of an idea by putting it into words.

One of my goals for revision is to communicate better with others. My successive drafts represent my efforts to take what I want to say and articulate it more clearly to someone else. My revision goal is often to revise for clarity. This goal combines a number of goals described earlier. I will reorganize the text so that the story line of the chapter is potentially more elegant. To make the chapter more illuminating, I will seek additional classroom examples. I will create additional tables and figures to make the text more illustrative. One of my limiting habits as a writer is that I compose longer sentences, which can obscure the point I want to make. Part of becoming more concise, for me, is at the sentence level. I consider which longer sentences need to be edited into two shorter sentences.

Even when I revise to improve the text to communicate with others, the process of revising continues to sharpen my own thinking about an idea. If I edit down a longer sentence into two sentences, I have to consider, *What do I really mean here?* Trying to write something more concisely pushes me to think about the essence of my point. Bringing in new examples or illustrations for an idea not only brings the idea to life for a reader but also helps me understand an idea as I consider why this example or that representation is appropriate to include. We continue to learn as we strive to communicate more clearly to others.

To help students become more metacognitive, share your own thought process. When students share how their thinking shifted, I am often open about how my own thinking shifted on the same topic. I want to model that we are all constantly learning. Sharing our revising processes with our students can help them feel validated about the changes in their own thinking and can normalize the bumpiness of the learning process.

Listening to Learn Through Revising

To revise our thinking, we need new insights to consider. It is difficult to revise without feedback, and it is difficult to give feedback unless we listen closely. Listening carefully to how others think can be inspiration to inform our revisions. Asking students to give feedback on peers' drafts presents a challenge and an opportunity—everyone can improve how we listen to one another. We can all learn to listen in supportive and empathetic ways. We all, students and teachers, benefit when we strive together to listen to understand rather than judge and co-generate new mathematical ideas together. Learning to listen to one another is not easy.

When we hear something that sounds different from how we currently think, what do we do? Do we shut down and think, *That doesn't make sense?* Instead, what we might think is, *This doesn't make sense to me right now because I'm not thinking in that way yet*. Even if a student's thinking misses the mark of what we hope they might say, there is likely to be at least a glimmer of a strong idea that the student can build on when they are revising their work.

Allison Hintz, Kersti Tyson, and Andrea English (2018) write about empathic listening. To listen with empathy, we listen to try to understand how someone else thinks. We actively suspend our own perspectives and ideas. We don't discard our own thinking; rather, we can put our thinking on hold for a bit while we entertain another way of thinking. This practice honors that someone else's ideas are worth taking into account. Both teachers and students benefit from engaging in empathic listening.

Hintz and her colleagues (2018) write about how teachers can use supportive listening to support students as they learn to engage in empathic listening. As we listen to students talk with one another, we can discern when students become supportive to one another. We can encourage students who are already supportive and position those students as models to one another. While we listen to make sense of students' thinking, we simultaneously listen to develop a classroom culture of supportive, empathic listening.

Evaluating

When we encourage students to share their rough draft thinking, there is a balance between creating a safe space for their thinking to land and challenging students to keep growing. I wouldn't want my thinking or my students' thinking to remain in a rough draft state. I hope for continued evolution, even as I want students to recognize value in their emerging ideas.

At the end of the semester at the university where I teach, there are opportunities for my students, who are studying to be teachers, to reflect on their experience in the course. I asked them to consider what instructional experiences supported their learning, so they can consider doing something similar with their students. My stance toward Nikki's thinking supported her learning:

> You always gave feedback that built off of what we'd already done rather than trying to change our ideas. It was like you were trying to help us build our ideas and make them better, rather than, "You should completely change this, and do something else." I always felt comfortable coming to you to talk through something because I knew you wouldn't attack the idea, and you'd help me make it better.
>
> —Nikki, preservice elementary teacher

I don't always communicate my intentions to my students as well as I would like. But in this case, I was thrilled that Nikki had this experience with feedback from me. This is the kind of evaluation I hope to give: to first seek to understand how someone thinks, to identify strengths in those emerging ideas, and to support the student in building on those ideas to take them further.

What is the role of assessment? Is it to sort the best from the not-quite-good-enough submissions? Instead, it could be to identify opportunities to grow and to build on current states of thinking.

During mathematics lessons, I wonder when it is appropriate to take an evaluative stance on students' thinking. I want students to feel safe to share their thinking. I will sometimes collect ideas and then pause rather than comment, whether or not the idea would benefit from refinement. If I stop talking, students will often correct themselves and one another, ask clarifying questions of one another, or add on to one another's thinking for elaboration.

This all makes me wonder: What counts as an evaluation, anyhow? Highlighting and validating students' productive ways of thinking is a form of evaluating. Noticing and identifying aspects of someone's thinking is a form of judging it in some way, because we shine a light on what is valuable for attention and consideration. But perhaps some evaluations are less threatening than others.

Do students have opportunities to revise tests and quizzes in the mathematics classroom? Should they? If they do not, how do the classroom assessment practices relate to creating a culture where rough drafts can be a part of ongoing learning? In Chapters 5 and 6, I reflect on assessment further. But I do want to share that I have some ambivalence about graded tests and quizzes. Tests and quizzes capture what students are thinking at one point in time. They measure performance, potentially both procedural skill and conceptual understanding. However, I also care about growth in understanding and mastery of concepts. I conjecture that standards-based grading and portfolio assessments would be practices that align well with rough draft thinking. Standards-based grading promotes the notion that students are constantly working toward understanding particular concepts. Portfolios allow for students to reflect on and demonstrate how their thinking grew.

We Are All Works in Progress

Being constantly open to revision while engaging in rough draft thinking is living on the edge. It's the space between certainty and debilitating doubt. When I can get comfortable with engaging in rough draft thinking and sharing it with others, I am able to embrace that I am good enough as I am. Ideally, we want students to see that their current ideas have potential and are worth sharing and working on. We want students to have the bravery to value their emerging thoughts. But we also hope that they have the humility to desire to continue growing and changing. Doubts in emerging thoughts can be facilitative if we let go of a need to be correct and instead strive for continued evolution. Letting go of uncertainty is a challenge for everyone. There is safety in feeling like we've reached a destination in our knowledge. But there is beauty in constantly growing our knowledge.

Kathleen Wilson (from the Talking Points example discussed earlier) said that she tries to encourage her students to get comfortable with being uncomfortable. She often uses the metaphor of seeds being planted.

> When students' thinking is "rough," I say that we are planting seeds. As we work to get a deeper understanding, we are fertilizing and watering the idea until it flourishes. So the emerging ideas are the seeds from which it all starts. You can't

> grow anything without having that first seed of an idea. So, just as you stated that you wouldn't want students' thinking to stay in a rough state, neither would we want our flower to stay a seed that never sprouts beyond a seed. I reference this idea quite a bit, especially when I can see that students seem uncomfortable with something new. Then I'll remind them that they felt that way about other things once as well. "Remember when we first learned the unit circle? It seemed very rough at first, but now you all truly understand it and it makes sense. Don't worry, we'll get there with this idea, too."
>
> —Kathleen Wilson, high school math teacher

Kathleen said that, at least once a week, she reminds students that their rough ideas are the start of something great, and she helps them see that ideas that they understand now once started in a rougher state.

Through revising, we refine our thinking. We are not replacing a broken idea with a fixed one. We are taking something that has potential and bringing it into its full possibility.

It's radical to engage in revision regularly in mathematics classrooms. As we start to believe that our thinking about mathematics can constantly evolve, we shift our thinking about what mathematical knowledge is and what it means to come to know mathematics. Maybe I already think I know how to solve problems with right triangles using trigonometry, but my thinking about why trigonometry makes sense can continue to grow and shift. I can make new connections between the graphical representations of a trigonometric function and a unit circle. We never stop making sense of mathematics as we keep thinking about it.

We are all works in progress. That's not a weakness. That's amazing. Mathematical thinking is limitless. So, let's keep revising our thinking about doing math and our thinking about teaching math.

CHAPTER FIVE

ROUGH DRAFT THINKING AS A REHUMANIZING ENDEAVOR

I long for students' fears of sharing their thinking about math to become uncommon. In this chapter, we'll look more closely at classrooms where teachers have successfully created humanized spaces by promoting rough draft thinking. When teachers work with some of the instructional approaches and perspectives described in this book, students feel valued as people. As we learn from teachers at work, we'll explore the relationship between teaching rough draft math and humanizing mathematics classrooms.

Suzi Sappington's Humanized High School Classroom

> I never used to want to share in class and I was always incredibly anxious to be randomly called on. Now I always want to share because I feel comfortable here.
>
> —Tina, tenth grade, white female student, Appoquinimink High School

Suzi Sappington teaches Integrated Math 3 honors at Middletown High School, and Tina is one of her students. Suzi has been teaching for seven years, and she has taught at the same high school for the past five years. I asked her to share what she thought happened in her classroom that led to Tina expressing these thoughts.

SUZI SAPPINGTON'S CONJECTURES ABOUT HOW SHE HUMANIZES HER CLASSROOM

- No cold calling
- Build relationships by listening to students
- Anonymous sharing
- Model vulnerability

Suzi shared a few conjectures: eliminating cold calling, building relationships with students by listening and responding to them, providing opportunities for sharing anonymously, and modeling vulnerability. These four approaches combined to create a mathematics classroom where students like Tina felt comfortable, not anxious.

Eliminate Cold Calling

The decision to cut cold calling came from her students. When Suzi asked her students to brainstorm rights they wanted to have as learners in her classroom (discussed in Chapter 2), students in this class period asked for *the right to not publicly share*. Students asked for the right to choose not to share if they were called on and the choice to share when they wanted to share.

At first, Suzi was concerned that this right would lead to a silent classroom, but she continued to reflect. She said, "Then I thought about it some more. You don't want to force responses. You don't want to make someone talk who doesn't want to talk. I tried to honor that." She hoped that students would feel more comfortable to share with the class if they had time to work in groups first. To honor their request, "it did take some willpower on my part if I know that a student has a great idea, but it might not be something she feels comfortable sharing publicly."

The day Tina told Suzi that she felt comfortable in the classroom, Tina had participated a lot, "basically walking us [the class] through the whole warm-up." After class, Suzi approached Tina to thank her for sharing her thinking that day. During this conversation, Tina told Suzi about her experiences in other math classrooms. Previously, if her math teacher asked her to be ready to be called on at any time, Tina used to think, "Ugh, it's gonna be me . . . it's gonna be me," and that anticipation produced a lot of stress for her. Tina expressed that she felt safer in Suzi's class.

Build Relationships by Listening to Students

Suzi believed that the relationship she had built with Tina made a difference for Tina. Suzi said, "She [Tina] and I connected. I know that sometimes students don't connect with other teachers." Suzi recognized that students might clash with their teacher in ways that make them feel like they do not want to share in the classroom. Part of building relationships with students is taking their ideas seriously. For Suzi, this included honoring the rights that students requested.

Anonymous Sharing

Students may first need to try sharing aloud anonymously to see how it goes before they feel comfortable sharing their own work publicly. One example from Suzi's classroom was when they thought about trinomials where the a value was not equal to one ($ax^2 + bx + c$). Suzi created a "shout it out" such that students could anonymously enter ideas from their Chromebooks into Desmos so that they would appear on the whiteboard.

Suzi wanted students to explore how the same expression could be written in equivalent ways. She gave students an expression, and she had them enter how they could write out the trinomial in factored forms. The class discussed similarities and differences among the student-generated examples. For instance, Suzi provided the class with this expression: $4x^2 + 11x + 6$. Some students wrote $(x + 2)(4x + 3)$, while others saw that you would also be able to write it as $4(x + 2)(x + \frac{3}{4})$. Anonymous sharing allowed Suzi to recognize and acknowledge students' thinking as contributions without students being in the spotlight. Using Desmos, Suzi was able to see who shared which contribution, although the students could not tell who shared, and she could strategically decide whose ideas to amplify.

Suzi conjectured that, when students' thinking was positioned as valuable in an anonymous way, those students would start sharing more publicly in the future.

Model Vulnerability with Students

> What I try to do is be very transparent about not knowing things and to share my personal experiences in math. A lot of times, I'll share with my students that I didn't really know what I was doing in high school. I kind of just followed what my teachers told me to do, and I did it, and then you get your grade and you're done. You know, I truly didn't understand math until I started teaching it.
>
> —Suzi Sappington, high school math teacher

In Suzi's classroom, students' rights include *the right to make mistakes* and *the right to revise your thinking*. Suzi acknowledges when she needs to exercise those rights, too. "I was teaching the method of undetermined coefficients last week, and I was just making errors left and right, because it's tedious. You have to solve a three-variable system using substitution. Any one miscalculation throws the whole system off. My students were being so gracious saying, 'I think there needs to be a 3 there, maybe a 6.' I thanked them for correcting my errors in a polite way and I acknowledged that I make mistakes as well."

She said that, if you can be vulnerable with your students, "it shows that you're being honest with them. You're not trying to put on some character. And then they can be real themselves. And then students like Tina can feel, okay, I can share. I can share my ideas. I can share my thoughts. Because you know Mrs. Sappington's being real. She's not judging us. She just wants to share what we have to say."

Suzi wondered if Tina felt more pressure because of being labeled as an "honors" student. Then, she also realized that perhaps she also could check her own assumptions about students in an honors section. "You put that stereotype on the student you're going to get in these honors classes. But it makes me want to step back. Should I have these predisposed ideas about who I am going to have in this classroom?" Suzi considered that labeling students in these ways could create unhelpful expectations.

She also wondered if students make assumptions about teachers of honors students. "Sometimes I do fear that they have expectations of an honors teacher—that their teacher needs to be perfect all of the time." She thought some of these expectations would be: *Oh, they always have it put together. They have the most rigorous and engaging activities. They're at a higher level all of the time*. Is this tracking of teachers, too? I've had moments in my planning where I'm just, ugh, I don't think I'm good enough for this! I need to take a dose of my own medicine. I might not be perfect all of the time, but I'm just going to keep at it and keep reflecting."

Connections to Rough Draft Thinking

Although Suzi did not say that she had students revise, it was apparent to me that a spirit of rough draft thinking was alive in how she engaged with students. Anonymous sharing welcomes students' ideas at any stage. Students feel freer to treat sharing as brainstorming rather than as performing correctness because they get to be anonymous. Suzi's school is one-to-one, with all students having Chromebooks checked out to them, and anonymous sharing through tools such as Desmos, Padlet, or Google Docs is one way to capitalize on the technology.

Suzi encourages her students and herself to view themselves as works in progress. Suzi is constantly trying to accept herself and her students as they are right now, while challenging herself and her students to grow further. Her reflection helped me think about how I, as a teacher and as a person, need to do the work of being honest with myself and my students if I want them to take intellectual risks with me.

Humanizing the Mathematics Classroom: My Early Draft

What does it mean to humanize the classroom? Because I think the instructional routine of Stronger and Clearer Each Time (Zwiers et al. 2017) is a helpful rough draft thinking routine for students, I am going to engage in the practice for myself. I will draft an initial definition, informed by Suzi's conjectures about supporting Tina and her other students and informed by my own reading. By reflecting on other teachers' classrooms and academic texts, I can, then, work on a revised definition throughout the chapter and connect that definition to rough draft thinking.

Here's my first draft: The word *human* is embedded in humanizing, so humanizing the mathematics classroom must be *making the classroom a place where students can be fully themselves.*

When a classroom is humanized, students do not have to check their past histories and ways of being outside of school at the door. Their lived experiences and ideas are resources that support their learning, their classmates' learning, and their teachers' ongoing learning.

Humanizing the mathematics classroom is an ongoing process, so in mathematics classrooms, students are not only experiencing opportunities to learn content but also learning regularly about how they can be, as people who do mathematics (or not), in that classroom and beyond. Students develop their identities as they develop concepts and skills in mathematics classrooms. Julia Aguirre, Karen Mayfield-Ingram, and Danny Martin (2013) provide a helpful definition of identity:

> "We define mathematics identity as the dispositions and deeply held beliefs that students develop about their ability to participate and perform effectively in mathematical contexts and to use mathematics in powerful ways across the contexts of their lives. Depending on the context, a mathematics identity may reflect a sense of oneself as a competent performer who is able to do mathematics or as the kind of person who is unable to do mathematics" (14).

Inspired by this definition, another part of my current draft is that, in a *humanized mathematics classroom, students' thoughts and actions are seen as contributions toward ongoing learning and sense-making for themselves, their peers, and their teacher.*

Humanize by Seeing Students as Capable People

To push my working definition onward in my current draft, I continued reading. I encountered this stance on humanizing mathematics classrooms: *Seeing students as people who are capable of learning who bring productive ways of thinking to the activity of doing mathematics, "not collections of deficits or skill gaps"* (Lambert et al. 2018, 129). All students deserve opportunities to wonder using mathematics as a way of thinking, whether or not the students are identified as honors students or as benefiting from special education accommodations, no matter what their histories of prior achievement. To value rough draft thinking is to value the ideas that students have and offer to the class.

It is dangerous to wait to give students a chance to engage in rough draft thinking until we think that they are ready for it. We might think that only some students can work on developing their understandings through talking or writing, revisiting, and revising. Rough draft thinking is not only for the "high fliers." (Note: I write the phrase "high flier," but I don't actually believe that such a category exists. I just hear some people using this phrase. But all students are capable of enacting some form of mathematical smartness. Every student is capable of flying high about some aspect of mathematical thinking.)

It's also dangerous to view rough draft thinking as only an intervention to support "struggling students." (Again, "struggling students" is not a label I think exists. Everyone struggles when learning anything new. We are all learners, and we all struggle through making sense of things.) Although, yes, rough draft thinking does help support students to engage in productive struggling, everyone benefits from treating their mathematical work as rough drafts. Students in honors classes, like Tina in Suzi's classroom, feel relief—as if air is let out of a pressure balloon—if they aren't expected to be perfect all of the time and if learning is treated as a process of continual evolving.

To update my draft definition: Humanizing the mathematics classroom is *making the classroom a place where students can be fully themselves. In a humanized mathematics classroom, students experience that their teachers view them as capable learners and doers of mathematics. Students' thoughts and actions are seen as contributions toward ongoing learning and sense-making for themselves, their peers, and their teacher.*

When a classroom has a spirit of rough draft thinking, teachers welcome students' voices and create spaces that invite more students to feel safe sharing those ideas.

We might be nervous to open up the floor to hear students' ideas because when anyone learns something new, the thinking can sound like it is all over the place. It might even sound to us like our students are confusing themselves. But it is better to listen to students' ideas so we can participate with them in the evolution of their ideas. When we take the time to really listen to students, their ideas can inspire us. Let's visit another classroom to see how.

Tom Becker's Humanized Mathematics Classroom

> Someone may say that they know more than me, but that doesn't make them greater than I am or more valuable to the world than I am. Understanding that I don't have to know everything, that I still have a right to learn, and I am just as an important human being and just as smart and capable as anybody else—that's what's important.
>
> —Jasmine, eleventh grade, Black female student, MOT Charter High School

I wish that all students would see themselves as important human beings who are smart and capable, including and especially during mathematics class, like Jasmine does.

Jasmine is one of Tom Becker's Integrated Math 4 students at Middletown-Odessa-Townsend Charter in Middletown, Delaware. Tom has been teaching for ten years, and he has been teaching with the *Interactive Mathematics Program (IMP)* curriculum materials for nine years. This past year, he was selected as one of the teachers of the year for the state of Delaware. Tom reflected with me about rights of learners in his classroom and instructional choices he makes that humanize his classroom and support rough draft thinking, which may have contributed to Jasmine's thinking.

Three of the strategies he described were (1) promoting mutual respect among students, (2) revising a unit problem to reflect on evolving ideas, and (3) providing choice for how to demonstrate knowledge on a performance assessment.

TOM BECKER'S STEPS TO HUMANIZE HIS MATH CLASSROOM

- Promoting mutual respect
- Revising a unit problem
- Choice of format for performance assessment

Promoting Mutual Respect Among Students

Tom promoted rights of learners in his classroom, which were discussed in Chapter 2. On the second day of school, Tom asked his students to generate a list about what they thought their rights as learners should be. Students wrote, listed, and displayed their ideas about possible rights all over the room.

The classes then discussed comparisons among the rights and determined the underlying ideas about what was important to them. Tom said,

> What our discussion really came around to was that every single right the kids came up with was about being judged. The underlying feeling was, they don't want to be judged. Everything that we talk about it, was that a judgment statement, was that not a judgment statement? That's what the result of this is. We got so far as saying, someone said, *That's easy*. That's not allowed to be said in my classroom anymore, because we consider that judging someone.

—Tom Becker, high school math teacher

To enforce this perspective of withholding judgment, Tom emphasized not judging on a daily basis. He encouraged students to instead try to understand one another rather than evaluate one another. Near the end of the first quarter or marking period, he had students reflect and write about their experiences with their rights in the mathematics classroom. He gave the students a questionnaire:

- Are you respecting each other's rights in the classroom?
- Is Mr. Becker respecting your rights?
- Do you feel like your rights are being respected?
- Explain your thoughts.

Out of 185 students, only 3 said that they did not feel like their rights were being respected. Tom has been reaching out to these three students. In conversation with them, two of the students prefer teaching styles that differ from his. One student said that he is looking for more direct instruction, and another student admitted that she did not feel comfortable asking questions. The third student felt frustrated because when he tried to help people, they got mad at him.

Tom's instructional approach puts responsibility on the students to ask questions about what they want to understand next.

> My class normally runs, like, they start a problem and work on it individually, then with each other. They ask each other questions. I'll go around and see what they're doing. They'll ask questions. They'll answer questions. They really work together by asking each other questions. *What are you doing? How did you do that? That doesn't make sense to me*. But if you don't feel comfortable asking questions when you're confused, you have a really hard time in my class. That's what I think is happening to two of those kids. They get confused and stuck, and they're not asking their groupmates for help. Or they're not asking for clarification when their groupmate says something to them. They're not understanding it, and they're not asking again. They're just saying, *Oh, okay*. And they're going back to their work.
>
> —Tom Becker

When Tom circulates the room during group work, he first tries to understand what each group is thinking by seeing what they're doing. He pushes them to ask one another questions and to answer one another's questions. He asks them questions and provides certain clarifications if they're helpful. Then, to push each group, he tries to leave each table with a question. To start the second marking period, he planned to have a conversation around their reflection responses by sharing common trends in students' thinking about their rights in the classroom.

Revising a Unit Problem

Tom's mathematics units are thematic. They are grounded in a unit problem that introduces students to the chapter, and the investigations throughout the chapter support students with making progress on subsets of ideas and skills that allow them to make more progress on the unit problem. Multiple mathematics curriculum series are structured this way to some degree, such as *Connected Mathematics Project* in middle grades, and Tom's school uses *IMP* in high school.

Tom said, "At the very beginning of the year, the very first day of class, we tried the unit problem, which was the *Ferris Wheel* problem" (Fraser, Fendel, and Resek 2011). In this problem, students were asked to think about a moving Ferris wheel with a tub of water running along on a track under it. A person wants to dive off of the moving wheel just in time to land in the cart. Students came up with ideas. Tom said, "We had a classroom poster that had all of their ideas on it. We recorded all of those thoughts." Through brainstorming, students also had to consider what assumptions they needed to make to work on the task. The poster remained up in the room while students were working on the unit. Tom handled the problem so that rough draft ideas were framed as conjectures. This process got students wondering about the task and the ideas in it.

Throughout the unit, students then worked on related activities set in other contexts to help them make sense of the mathematics in the unit problem. After working on these related activities, students then encountered a modified version of the unit problem, with more information about the Ferris wheel, to decide more precisely when (at what time) the assistant should let the diver go for the diver to land in the cart. Their poster of initial, rough draft ideas was displayed so students could compare and contrast their first ideas with their new ones.

The chance to revisit and revise thinking on a challenge problem is a humanizing endeavor. It acknowledges that challenging tasks can and should take a long time to solve. Taking a while to make progress on a task counteracts the prevailing idea that we are either smart at math or we're not and the smart people can figure out a problem right away. Instead, a way to enact our mathematical smartness is by taking our time to make sense out of something and pursuing related questions to help us answer a larger question.

Choice of Format for Performance Assessment

Tom asked his students to revise their thinking about the unit problem as a performance assessment. He said that it was important to revisit the unit problem: "We had been working on individual skills that would help them with their unit problem, but they hadn't put everything together yet." Given the following information, students had to determine at what time to release the diver:

FERRIS WHEEL:

- Starts at the 3 o'clock position
- Takes 40 seconds to rotate
- Radius = 50 feet
- Height from the ground to the center is 65 feet
- Ferris Wheel moves counter-clockwise

CART:

- The tub is 8 feet above the ground
- 240 feet to the left of the center of the Ferris wheel
- Moves 15 feet per second

For this opportunity to revise their thinking about the unit problem, Tom invited his students to use the format of their choice. "What I told them was—I want you to create a video or a PowerPoint or something. They could have made a paper. They were trying to put everything together to solve the unit problem again." Students completed the assessment in groups. As an example, he shared a video with me of students standing at a wall with a series of large posters on the wall. The students explained their thinking about all of the parts of the unit problem and how they could be integrated to solve the problem.

When given the choice to make a video about their thinking, Tom said, "They [students] really like that. They really catch on to it. I give them options. They could do a video or they could do a PowerPoint. I probably get about half and half." The second time in the semester when he had students do a performance assessment like this, he received even more videos.

After I watched more videos of his students' thinking, I noticed that students not only had posters on the walls but also had literally written on the walls with whiteboard markers. Tom said that many of the walls throughout the school, not just in classrooms, but in hallways and other common spaces, were painted with whiteboard paint. In Tom's classroom, he didn't have whiteboard paint on his walls, so his students could go out into the hallway to work on their math projects or any other group work from math class, work that remained on the hallways of the school for a time. This felt like a great way to display ongoing mathematical thinking—putting our thinking in progress out for all to observe.

Tom also shared another way that he incorporates video into asking students to show what they know, formatively. He wanted students to have access to one another's thinking at home. "I will have them try a problem or have different groups try different problems, and I'll have them videotape themselves doing it, and then they'll upload them to discussion boards, and they'll have access to those videos. They can then watch those problems over and over again to prepare for a test. That's how I started doing these videos."

I was curious about how Tom graded the performance assessments. He said, "I like grading it more. I can tell what the kids are doing, how they're thinking. It's more fun to watch." He then said that he had to write "a creative rubric that allows me to grade pretty much any way they can do it. The rubric is about the content." Portions of the rubric he used are shown in Table 5.1.

PART OF TOM'S RUBRIC FOR EVALUATING STUDENTS' PERFORMANCE ASSESSMENTS

With a group, create a visually appealing presentation that fully explains each formula in detail. Some suggested formats are video, PowerPoint, Prezi, or a detailed paper.

In your presentation, explain each of the formulas that represent (1) the diver's height, (2) the diver's x-coordinate, (3) the free-fall time, (4) the cart's distance equation. Explain how each of the pieces of the Ferris wheel fit into the formulas. Once you explain a piece once, you do not have to explain it again. Be sure to discuss the triangles inside the Ferris wheel throughout your explanation of your first two formulas.

Attempt to solve the unit problem. In your presentation, discuss a plan to solve the unit problem. Try to solve the unit problem. Submit your work along with what you believe the solution is. Remember, the solution is the time that the diver should let go of the Ferris wheel.

Criteria	**Grading Scale**			
The Diver's Height	**3**	**2**	**1**	**0**
Presentation includes: equation of the diver's height, an explanation of how the equation was created using a triangle, and an explanation of where the numbers in the equation came from in terms of the Ferris wheel.	There is a correct equation to determine the height of the diver. There is a detailed explanation of how the equation was created using a triangle. There is an explanation of where the numbers in the equation came from in terms of the Ferris wheel. There are minimal errors and no pieces of missing information.	There is an equation included to determine the height of the diver. There is a detailed explanation of how the equation was created using a triangle. There is an explanation of where the numbers in the equation came from in terms of the Ferris wheel with 1-3 errors or 1-2 pieces of missing information.	There is an equation included to determine the height of the diver with more than 3 errors in the equation or explanation. OR There is a correct equation included to determine the height of the diver with no explanation about how the equation was created.	There is not a correct equation provided to determine the height of the diver. There is no attempt to explain how such an equation would be determined.

TABLE 5.1

Tom provided a similarly detailed rubric for the other three formulas the students were expected to explain. The rubric also contained expectations for mechanics of writing (Table 5.2).

TOM'S RUBRIC TO ASSESS MECHANICS

Criteria	Grading Scale			
Creativity/ Grammar/Editing The presentation is organized. All equations and words can be read easily or heard on video. All scenes/slides are edited. The presentation is visually appealing.	**3** The presentation is well organized. All equations and words can be read easily or heard on video. All scenes/slides are edited. The presentation is visually appealing.	**2** The presentation is organized. Most equations and words can be read easily or heard on video. Most scenes/slides are edited. The presentation is visually appealing.	**1** There is an attempt at organization. Most equations and words can be read or heard on video.	**0** There is no apparent attempt at organization. The equations and words in the presentation are difficult to read or hear.

TABLE 5.2

Tom intended to design the rubric so that students would get credit for their effort to articulate their thinking. The students' grades were not based only on the correctness of their solutions.

I wondered whether editing the videos was intimidating for students. He said that the students had been prepared to do this kind of work. The juniors and seniors in his classes had learned how to edit videos during a computer class that they had taken during their freshman year. The school is one-to-one; all students have Chromebooks.

Providing students with opportunities to express themselves using multiple modalities, such as video, is humanizing. Giving students a choice promotes agency. Allowing students to video-record their thinking gives them a chance to express their voices. Hearing students talk about their ideas feels more personal than reading their work. If students share their videos, they support one another's learning in community, and they come to value their peers' thinking and the opportunity to share their own thinking. If students have lots of opportunities and spaces to express and explore their thinking beyond worksheets and textbook problems, doing mathematics becomes more playful.

Connections to Rough Draft Thinking

Part of the spirit of a rough draft classroom is focusing on trying to understand one another rather than judging one another. When we learn from our rough drafts, we are not focused on performing in ways that lead to evaluation; instead, we are oriented toward constantly learning together. The rights of learners allowed students to focus on not judging one another negatively so that they could instead learn to listen to one another.

Revisiting thinking about a challenging task is a great example of the spirit of rough drafts in the mathematics classroom. The *Ferris Wheel* problem was interesting and challenging enough that it was worth thinking through another time. Students could compare their initial ideas to their current thinking to see the evolution of their ideas.

To Humanize Honors the Dignity in One Another

As I continued my reading about humanizing the mathematics classroom, I encountered the work of Andrew Brantlinger (2018). Brantlinger considered the meaning of *humanizing*, citing Ericson, who suggested that although it might not be clear what humanizing means, it could be easier to understand through its opposite: dehumanizing, or "the denial of dignity of the individual" (quoted in Ericson 1991, 31). Brantlinger (2018) connects this idea to critical pedagogical practices, saying that we humanize our teaching when we value and seek multiple worldviews, representing a range of cultures and races and communities, and welcome nonstandard ways of thinking and being in the classroom. Also, he writes that critical educators position students as authorities in relation to mathematics, so that they recognize that mathematics is human-made, fallible, and that they can contribute to making new mathematical knowledge or, as Freudenthal (1991) said, reinvent mathematical knowledge. Humanizing the classroom is a process that must be constantly constructed and reconstructed to honor students' dignity.

In Tom's room, the dignity of students was amplified by students' efforts to continually treat one another with mutual respect. They strove to take one another's thinking seriously. Tom valued their thinking at all stages and created structures so that students could learn from one another (videos to share their thinking with peers, for instance). Tom sought multiple ways of thinking and being through alternative forms of assessments in which students could express their thinking in ways that made sense to them.

It's the idea of honoring the dignity of every student that resonates with me. My definition should be updated to include this idea:

Humanizing the mathematics classroom is *making the classroom a place where students can be fully themselves and where the dignity of each and every student is honored. In a humanized mathematics classroom, students experience that their teachers view them as capable learners and doers of mathematics. Students' thoughts and actions are seen as contributions toward ongoing learning and sense-making for themselves, their peers, and their teacher.*

I appreciated that even though 182 of his students reported that their rights were being respected, Tom focused on trying to understand the other three students. He wasn't satisfied with 98 percent of his students experiencing respect. All students deserve to have their dignity honored.

Shellee Wong's Humanized Mathematics Classroom

It would be wonderful if all students left math class feeling like this student:

> You make me feel like a somebody, Miss Wong.
>
> —Allison, tenth grade, white female student, Middletown High School

Shellee Wong is a teacher at Middletown High School in Middletown, Delaware. She has been teaching for five years, and she has spent the past two years at this school teaching Integrated Math 3 and 4, including honors sections. Allison shared that she felt like a somebody in Shellee's classroom as part of a larger conversation in which some students observed that Shellee doesn't have favorites in her classroom. Students said that Shellee makes them feel smart just for asking a question.

When I asked Shellee to explain why she thought her student felt this way, like a somebody, Shellee told me stories of how she worked to build norms in her classroom and the power of letting students revise their tests.

SHELLEE WONG'S STEPS TO HUMANIZE HER MATH CLASSROOM

- Explicit reflection on norms
- Building norms over time
- Revising assessments

Explicit Reflection on Norms to Promote Rough Draft Thinking

When you walk into Shellee's classroom, many inspiring words are hung on the walls, such as her class theme of the year: "Be Brave. Be Kind." Right above the whiteboard in the front of the room, she hung a large poster that said, "Your ideas are the currency of the classroom." Other signs say:

> *Be confused. It's where you begin to learn new things.*
>
> *Be broken. It's where you begin to heal.*
>
> *Be frustrated. It's where you start to make more authentic decisions.*
>
> *Be sad. Because if we are brave enough, we can hear our heart's wisdom through it.*
>
> *Be whatever you are right now. No more hiding. You are worthy. Always.*

These are not simply slogans for Shellee. She works with her students to make sense out of what they mean in her classroom. She also kicked off her semester with the same process used by Tom and Suzi: introducing rights of learners and brainstorming new ones. She began with the five rights of learners (to be confused, to make a mistake, to say what makes sense to you, to share unfinished thinking and not be judged, and to revise your thinking).

Early in the semester, she helped students make sense of these rights by engaging them in an instructional routine, Contemplate-then-Calculate (Kelemanik and Lucenta 2019) during which students were asked to share different ways of seeing and counting the total number of dots in the dot pattern in Figure 5.1. Shellee had a purpose of asking students to share many ways of seeing the dot pattern. "I wanted the students to understand, *What does this look like in a math classroom? What does it mean to exercise your right? What does it mean when Miss Wong says, 'Be brave. Be kind.'?*"

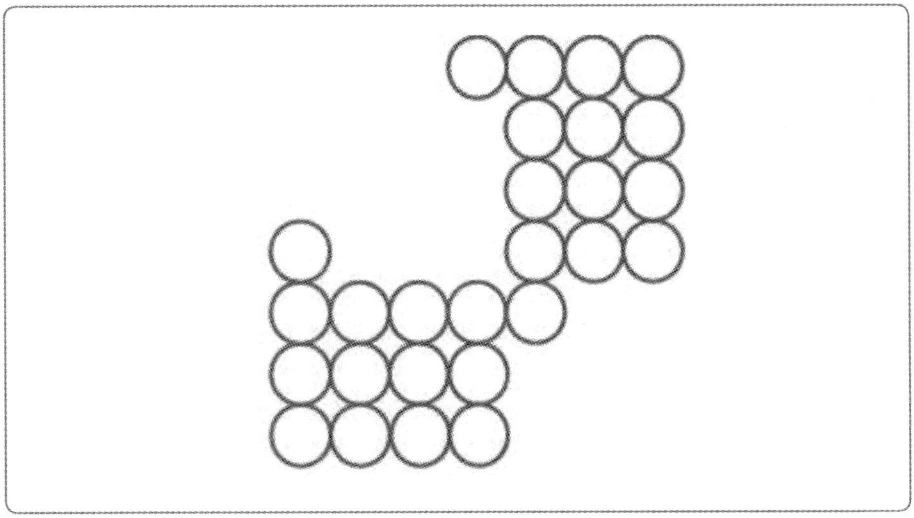

Figure 5.1
Dot Pattern from Kelemanik and Lucenta (2019)

While implementing the routine, she pointed out moments when students enacted their rights. To be explicit, Shellee observed which right was being exercised by a student, and she amplified that. She said, "I'm really sorry, but I am going to interrupt you multiple times throughout this exercise for the sake of making things explicit." According to Shellee, it was by the second class that a student noticed that peers were picking up on naming rights. Students participated and said things like, "Yes! You reserve your right to make a mistake!" when a peer erased her answer and said that the total was 24 and not 27.

After she provided an explicit opportunity for students to engage in enacting their rights, Shellee asked students to brainstorm additional rights: "Are there any other rights you feel like you deserve as a learner that maybe are not captured by these five?" She took all of students' additional rights to heart:

- *The right to hold each other accountable when you see someone else violating each other's rights.* Students asked to call on another out if they were not abiding by these rights or if they are not aware that their rights are being violated. They wanted to promote the culture of, hey, we're all learning something new here, and it's okay to share in-progress or imperfect thinking.

- *The right to ask for more time when we feel like we all need it.* Some of her students had experiences with teachers in the past who would say, "You should have known this by now." Shellee was hesitant about giving students the right to request more time to learn at first. She wondered how to stay on pace for taking assessments in a timely manner. According to Shellee, students said that if they knew about the test a week in advance, "We'll do our part to meet that deadline, but in the process, if we need to slow down a day, are you willing to give up that time?" Because students realized that they had to put forth the effort before making this request, Shellee agreed to this right.

- *The right to understand other people's work ethics.* When Shellee asked her students to elaborate on what they meant by this, they would say that other students might seem to "get it" right away. It might seem like other students don't need to put in as much time to understand that certain concept. But if someone gets an A, no one knows if they put in seven hours to study for that grade or if they just happened to get an A without much effort. Strive not to judge someone else quickly. Strive not to assume you know whether they are working more or less hard than you are.

- *The right to politely dispute someone else's answer*. Shellee appreciated that the students requested this right, because it addresses mathematical practices about argumentation and attending to precision.

Shellee experienced that asking students to choose additional rights that they wanted to have was challenging. Shellee's students wanted to be able to ask for more time before taking an assessment. Truly honoring students' requests put Shellee in a position to transfer some control over to the students. Really humanizing the classroom to listen to students is not easy due to needing to let go of some of that control.

Shellee also invited students to reflect on other class norms. With respect to the "Be Brave. Be Kind." theme, Shellee shared with me that, in her experience, safe spaces can seem mythical. After all, no matter how "safe" the space supposedly is, it's still scary to share your thinking when you're not sure about it. Brave spaces made more sense to her than safe spaces. She asked her students about being brave and kind: "What does this mean to you? What does it look like in a math classroom?" They shared some of the following ideas:

- *Everyone's doing this for the first time, so if someone's going to be brave enough to share their answer, we'll be kind and we'll listen.*

- *I think being brave means trying the problem even when I initially think it's scary. Being brave enough to even try the problem.*

Giving students opportunities to reflect makes it more likely that these norms will have meaning for students.

Continuing to Build Norms

To establish norms, Shellee wanted to establish classroom interactions that aligned with the norms, so they were not just a slogan system. As early as the first day of the semester, Shellee said that students observed how nonverbal cues can violate people's rights. In reflecting on what it means to be kind, students observed that kindness or lack of kindness can appear in something as seemingly small as the look a teacher or peer gives when a student shares an answer. Shellee said that she shared aloud to her students, "I totally feel that on a very deep level. That happens all of the time when teachers are working on math together [in professional development], like, oh, you took a longer way than I would have solved it. 'Why would you do all of that? You could solve it this way.' But there are so many different ways! That's why I think at first students are resistant. 'Why is everyone sharing? Isn't there one right way? Can't you just give us the formula? Why are you making everyone share?' But everyone's mind is so beautiful. I want to feel exactly what you're thinking. Kids just look at me, like, 'What?!' But I'm being serious." Shellee goes beyond being neutral when students share, because she is genuinely enthusiastic about students' ideas.

Students supported one another when they enacted their rights throughout the semester. If a student would say, "I'm not sure that I'm right, but I'm exercising my right to try, anyway," peers would shout out, "It's okay!" Others would snap their fingers in encouragement and say, "We're all going to be kind." Students decided to reinforce the norms themselves.

Three weeks into the semester, Shellee then revisited these rights with students. She asked students to respond to some reflection questions: "How have you enacted your rights? What has been difficult about enacting your rights? When was a time when you changed your thinking?" One student response was, "It is challenging for me to enact my rights when I feel like everybody in the room already gets it and it's just me who has that one specific question." Indeed, it is an ongoing process to accept our own time frames for making sense of mathematics. This student also reflected that she could come in more for math help if she perceived that her peers were moving further along. Shellee also asked, "How have you already embraced the 'Be brave. Be kind.' theme? What more could you do to embrace this theme?" A student responded, "I should speak up more. Everyone seems like they're having fun."

Shellee constantly encouraged her students to recognize that learning doesn't always feel like succeeding. The process of learning can feel frustrating, so she would encourage her students to face that frustration directly.

I appreciated the ways that Shellee pushed her students to reflect on their experiences in class. Shellee's intended norms have more meaning for the students, and she received insights into her own students' experiences so that she could continue to support them.

Revising Assessments

Shellee knows that one thing that really matters to many high school students is their grade point average, so she decided to allow test corrections for all summative assessments in her class. Allowing for test corrections was a way that Shellee fully committed to giving students the right to revise their thinking. Students were taken aback at first or even shocked that they were allowed to correct their tests.

She gave her students this revision protocol: They had to submit the original answer, explain why it was marked incorrect, write out the correct answer, and explain why it is correct. Students could earn back up to half of the points that they lost on any test question. She gave students forty-eight hours after getting their tests back to complete the revisions.

Shellee referred to her unit assessments as *Celebrations of Knowledge*. A student said to her, "One thing I really love about you calling our unit assessments Celebrations of Knowledge is this nonpressure. I feel like I'm not pressured at all to have to get 100 percent. In an honors class, everyone is usually gunning to get that 100 percent, because you have to know it. With a Celebration of Knowledge, we're just celebrating whatever it is that we know at that time. You're giving us a chance to do test corrections about whatever we know, anyway. We can do them with you after school." After this particular student missed a month of school due to a life event, she was trying to catch up, so she decided just to take the Celebration of Knowledge to see how she would do.

Connections to Rough Draft Thinking

Listening to Shellee helped me think about how building a classroom culture to support rough draft thinking is an ongoing process. She and her students thought together about how listening and responding to one another can welcome or shut down the sharing of draft ideas. Her students helped me think about how it can be uncomfortable to share our work when we're not sure, but we can continually work with students to normalize and embrace these feelings.

It is an open question for me how the culture of assessments in a classroom can support or undermine a teacher's efforts to promote rough draft spaces where students can continually revise in-progress thinking. Shellee's protocol for revising tests seemed to fit well into a school where most teachers did not allow test revisions, because she did not allow students to earn all of the points back and she gave them a limited window for revising. The more I see teachers attempting to help students have rights related to developing and revising in-progress thinking, the more I see teachers pushing themselves to share authority with their students while changing their practices to consider the experiences of their learners.

Rehumanizing the Mathematics Classroom

To continue to think about what it might mean to humanize the mathematics classroom, I sought out the work of Rochelle Gutiérrez (2017, 2018). She helpfully casts the idea as rehumanizing what it means to do mathematics—in school and elsewhere. Schools and teachers can dehumanize the process of knowing and doing mathematics when we evaluate students in ways that do not honor the complexity of their thinking or appreciate the strengths in their thinking. We sometimes focus on control and domination of students rather than on giving students space to explore and wonder. School can teach students that they are only mathematical if they follow sanctioned ways of doing mathematics.

From reading and listening to Gutiérrez, I learned about some rehumanizing practices: it is helpful to move from listening for correct answers to appreciating various ways that students' think. I have thought about shifting from evaluating to interpreting, or seeking to understand, rather than finding deficits in students' thinking. Moving to appreciate students' thinking fits well into rough draft thinking. We can get excited about a way of thinking that we might not have thought about. We can spend time on how interesting it is to see the ideas from that lens and decide together how to build on that way of thinking.

Gutiérrez talks about rehumanizing mathematics as changing the game for students to go beyond improving achievement and access to mathematics toward embracing students' full selves—all parts of who they are. In an online lecture, she said,

> “Changing the game is not just thinking about how do we help more people be successful in the game, but how do we expect that new people who come into the field are going to ask different questions, are going to practice mathematics in different ways? And they are actually going to end up giving up and promoting a more vibrant version of mathematics because it is going to attend to this diversity of worldviews.” (Gutiérrez, 2018)

What mathematics is can be improved and revised if we embrace wider ways of knowing from our students and one other. These ideas in Table 5.3 about dehumanized and rehumanized mathematics were inspired by Gutiérrez's work:

MOVING FROM DEHUMANIZED MATHEMATICS TO REHUMANIZED MATHEMATICS

Dehumanized Mathematics	Rehumanized Mathematics
Individual students' ways of reasoning are not solicited or valued. They are instead viewed as deficits to be critiqued and fixed.	Invite students to share their ways of reasoning about mathematics and appreciate their ways of reasoning.
The emotional experience of mathematics is stripped away or ignored.	Welcome discussions of emotions experienced when doing mathematics.
The teacher or text is the authoritative source of knowledge.	Students can (re)invent mathematics.
Only certain students get recognized as "good" at math: the fast students, students of the dominant race or culture.	Publicly appreciate and amplify multiple ways of being good at math other than finishing quickly, particularly from students who might otherwise be positioned as having low status.
Give students only one chance to be correct.	Offer revision opportunities, including on assessments.
Teach students to play the game of school.	Change the game of school mathematics.

TABLE 5.3

We can rehumanize mathematics by inviting rough draft thinking. As we treat learning as an iterative process—as if we are all constantly growing in our thinking—our in-progress ideas are seen as something to appreciate. We are all accepted, just as we are, however we currently think, but we revisit and revise our thinking to move forward and grow. In a rough draft thinking space, if all ideas have merit, all people have merit, and the opportunity to learn more about mathematics is expanded.

To update my draft definition: Rehumanizing the mathematics classroom is *making the classroom a place where students can fully be themselves and where the dignity of each and every student is honored. In a rehumanized mathematics classroom, students experience that their teachers view them as capable learners and doers of mathematics. Students' thoughts and actions are seen as contributions toward ongoing learning and sense-making for themselves, their peers, and their teacher. The group of students and their teacher learn more about mathematics than they otherwise would have because a wide range of ways of thinking and doing mathematics are welcomed and appreciated.*

Through reflecting on how rough draft math can humanize the mathematics classrooms, I have come to see how our rough draft spaces can create ways of valuing more people while simultaneously opening ourselves up to more ways of seeing and thinking about mathematics.

Cautious Points

If we are not careful, rough draft thinking can become another dehumanizing practice. Imani Goffney, a professor at the University of Maryland, gave a presentation called "From Oakland to Wakanda: Transforming Math Classrooms to Become Equitable and Empowering Spaces for Black and Brown Students" (Goffney 2019). Among other important ideas, in this talk she discussed both the power of rough draft talk for empowering students as well as the importance of being cautious about rough draft talk.

It is essential to notice which students are being positioned as having in-progress ideas compared to which students are named as having ideas that are further along. Goffney wisely pointed out that students of color should not be the only students positioned as being in a rough draft stage of thinking. If a student is regularly identified as being in a draft stage and not highlighted as having made progress, their opportunities for positive identity development can be limited.

It is also useful to consider what criteria we use to determine whether ideas are further along. Students have ways of knowing mathematics that are culturally bound. I remember when I taught seventh grade in Mesa, Arizona. A student stayed after school to ask me if she could use a long-division algorithm that she used to use in Mexico. I told her that she could use strategies if they made sense to her and helped her correctly find the solution. She taught me her strategy, and it worked. Of course, she could use it! If I believed that a final draft should look like the algorithm I knew, I may have been tempted to position this strategy as being in progress. I appreciated that my student educated me.

A last update to my draft definition: Rehumanizing the mathematics classroom is *making the classroom a place where students can fully be themselves and where the dignity of each and every student is honored. In a rehumanized mathematics classroom, students experience that their teachers view them as capable learners and doers of mathematics. Students' thoughts and actions are seen as contributions toward ongoing learning and sense-making for themselves, their peers, and their teacher. The group of students and their teacher learn more about mathematics than they otherwise would have because a wide range of ways of thinking and doing mathematics are welcomed and appreciated. The brilliance of students of color is amplified in a rehumanized mathematics classroom.*

Humanizing the mathematics classroom through rough draft talk requires monitoring how we position students and their thinking. I want to give every student opportunities to have their thinking valued and to be seen as someone whose thinking has evolved. I want to take care to notice whether and how I can empower students of all races, and I want to ensure I value the contributions of students of color.

CHAPTER SIX

PUTTING "IT" INTO PRACTICE . . . OR

WE ARE ALL WORKS IN PROGRESS

Carla Hood, a math coach in the Colonial School District in New Castle County, Delaware, asked to talk with me about supporting teachers to put rough draft thinking into practice in mathematics classrooms. She had good insights, and one of her questions was particularly helpful to me: *How often should we do it (rough draft talk)? Once a week? Twice a month?* As I reflected on her question, I decided that the answer depends on what the "it" is.

We can take different approaches to put rough draft thinking into practice:

APPROACHES TO IMPLEMENTING ROUGH DRAFT THINKING

Foster a spirit of rough drafting daily:

- Purposefully develop the classroom culture (Chapter 2)
- Select and implement math tasks to invite drafting and revising (Chapter 3)
- Rehumanize the process of learning mathematics (Chapter 5)

Improve rough drafts and refine mathematical thinking periodically, as needed:

- Provide explicit opportunities to revise (Chapter 4)

In Chapter 2, we saw that one approach to promote rough draft thinking is to purposefully develop our classroom cultures. In Chapter 3, we looked closely at the role of task selection and implementation strategies that invite exploratory talk and revision. Another approach to promote rough draft thinking is to give students *explicit* opportunities to revise their mathematical thinking, which I described in Chapter 4. Chapter 5 highlighted that these efforts all together can lead to rehumanizing the mathematics classroom. While approaches described in these chapters interact and overlap, the distinctions among them are significant. When I made a renewed effort to incorporate rough draft thinking into my own teaching of mathematics, creating explicit opportunities for revising (Chapter 4) felt different than addressing my classroom culture (Chapter 2) or selecting and implementing tasks to foster rough draft thinking (Chapter 3).

We might consider the "it" in rough draft thinking to be giving students explicit revision opportunities. Explicit revision opportunities ask students to step back to look at their work and attempt to improve it by creating a new version, as described in Chapter 4. Perhaps revising on paper doesn't happen every day.

However, the "it" in rough draft thinking can also be fostering *a spirit of rough drafting* as we work on mathematics each day. Part of fostering this spirit is helping students appreciate that we can learn from one another's thinking at any stage. Another part is when we create a desire to continually improve our mathematical thinking through sharing and collaborating with others. That's the "it" that I imagine happening all of the time, in both explicit and subtle ways.

I decided to reinvest in teaching with rough draft thinking when I recently taught a mathematics content course for future elementary teachers. During this course, prospective teachers develop conceptual understanding for rational number concepts and operations, such as why the invert and multiply algorithm makes sense when fractions are divided. Students also develop flexible strategies for engaging in proportional reasoning. The overall rationale for the course is for prospective teachers to develop meaning for mathematical procedures they know how to use but may not deeply understand yet. Indeed, every time I teach the course, my own mathematical understandings continue to evolve.

As I taught this course, I tried to enact what I learned from researching and writing this book. I have viewed the process of writing this book as curating every good idea I have learned from colleagues and collaborators working in K–12 classrooms who have been using rough draft thinking in their teaching and coaching. I view this book as amplifying what I have learned from these thoughtful professionals. The terms *rough draft thinking* and *rough draft talk* could be incorporated into math instruction in so many ways; there is no one way to do it. Rough draft thinking is a generative idea that inspires teachers to try many different approaches. I challenged myself: If I wanted to put into practice what I have learned from teachers who incorporate rough draft thinking into their mathematics lessons, what would I do?

Facing Impostor Syndrome When I Enacted Rough Draft Math

It turned out to be harder than I thought. I experienced what many of us often experience: pressure to cover a lot of content quickly, snow days, students who sought more teacher-directed explanations rather than student-led discussions, and a personal life event that left me in survival mode some of the time. It turned out that I didn't use all of the rough draft thinking techniques I wanted to use while teaching. I was frustrated, because if I couldn't put everything into practice myself, wouldn't that mean I was exposing myself as a fraud?

Then, I reminded myself that we are all works in progress. As long as I purposefully tried some of the ideas from my own book, that was better than not using any at all. After all, the ideas in this book were curated from many different people. No one teacher was implementing all of these strategies, so it's probably unrealistic to expect to use all of them myself. Students could still benefit from rough draft thinking if I tried a portion of these strategies.

The more I try, the more these teaching practices will become habitual. Change happens gradually over time, and initially my change efforts might not unfold as I hope. I remembered my habit of being extra hard on myself. Sometimes I set a bar for myself that is almost impossible to hurdle, and then I am disappointed with myself when I don't make it. Ideally, I want to have a growth mindset for myself as a teacher, but I am still working to develop one.

I decided that maybe my own perspective on how my course unfolded wasn't reliable. I focused on what I did not do, which was provide students with explicit revision opportunities as often as I intended. I planned to build in revision opportunities once a week or twice a month. I provided fewer explicit revision experiences than that, so I thought I did not do enough. But my students did not know what I did *not* do. My class of prospective teachers may have still learned something about rough draft thinking from what I *did*. I decided to check in with my students. Based on what the students said about their experiences in my class, I could look back on my teaching over the semester and clarify to myself which of my instructional choices seemed to promote rough draft thinking.

Let Students' Perspectives Provide Insight

I gave my students a note card at the end of the last day of class. On the front of the note card, I asked them to write something that they liked about the course and something they would change (plus/delta). In addition, on the back of the note card, I asked the students to respond to this question: *Why might a teacher encourage the use of rough drafts or rough draft thinking in mathematics classrooms?* I had already asked the students this same question on a survey before the semester started. Some of their responses are in Table 6.1.

ACCORDING TO PROSPECTIVE ELEMENTARY TEACHERS: *WHY MIGHT A TEACHER ENCOURAGE THE USE OF ROUGH DRAFTS OR ROUGH DRAFT THINKING IN MATHEMATICS CLASSROOMS?*

Responses from the Beginning of the Semester	Responses from the End of the Semester
To me, a rough draft is an initial piece of work or thought that is in need of improvement. I think a teacher encourages this in math class to show students that it is okay to be wrong sometimes, as long as you keep working to improve your methods and eventually get the correct answer. *When I think of a rough draft, I think of the initial ideas and getting them down on paper. These might be useful in math to learn different ways to approach a problem or to see what areas of a student's knowledge needs more work.* I feel that a rough draft helps us expand our knowledge of math and come up with new and different ways of solving problems. I think teachers use rough drafts because it helps students work out their math problems on their own and figure out what they did wrong and then fix it. *To me a rough draft is a piece of work that is unfinished and allows for initial thoughts to be written down on paper. A teacher would encourage their students to use rough drafts in a mathematics classroom so that students may see the process to reach the solution.*	Rough drafts are important in math because it shows a person's initial response to working on a problem. It also allows for students to see how to improve and further develop their thinking. *Rough drafts can help encourage collaboration and trying even though you might doubt yourself.* I like sharing rough drafts in math, especially when I am stuck because explaining my thought process can help me work through a problem and if I am stuck, a classmate can help guide me based on what I already have done. *A teacher might encourage rough drafts because it's okay to be wrong. You can start an idea and another classmate can help you finish that thought, or you can learn from mistakes.* I found that using rough drafts this year really helped me put my thoughts into words. Sometimes you can think you understand it but not actually understand what you're doing. Talking it through makes it make more sense.

TABLE 6.1

(continued)

It gives you a chance to interpret the problem in your own mind so that you can better understand the concepts. *Because it gives you a chance to think out your thoughts and look for ways to make them better and more efficient.* A rough draft is like a first attempt and is not always perfect, but the rough draft is needed to understand the thought process that it takes to get to the final draft.	*I think that rough draft thinking made everyone more comfortable with sharing thoughts at the document camera. It was helpful to hear people say, "I'm not really sure . . . but this is what I did," because sometimes I also was not really sure.* Thoughts are always changing, and ideas can always be further developed. *To get ideas out and to improve on what the student knows with the help of the class. Someone might be just as confused.* You can always add more detail.

TABLE 6.1

Reading these future teachers' observations about rough draft thinking in mathematics reassured me. It turned out that they held powerful ideas about rough draft thinking in mathematics class, even though I only enacted a portion of what I wanted to enact. I did not do everything I wanted to do, but I may have done enough. That's an important idea for me to keep in mind as I work on my own teaching. While I keep raising the bar on myself, I also want to see strengths in my work as a teacher. I can treat my efforts to improve my teaching as a process of drafting, and I will continue to revise my efforts.

My students' incoming ways of thinking about rough drafts in mathematics classrooms reminded me that the term itself—*rough draft thinking*—has meaning embedded in it. Their responses validated that their prior experiences with using rough drafts in other contexts, particularly language arts, provided a starting point for activating awareness about the value of rough draft thinking in mathematics classrooms. I was very drawn to this prospective teacher's incoming way of describing rough draft thinking: it "gives you a chance to think out your thoughts." I would love future teachers to view talking and writing in mathematics class as a tool for continued learning and discovery rather than performing. Their responses also highlighted the power of revision and continued improvement, as well as learning from false starts or mistakes. Using the term *rough drafts* in mathematics classrooms from time to time can develop students' awareness about learning through continual drafting of ideas.

I felt relief when I read my prospective teachers' outgoing perspectives on rough draft thinking, because they revealed that students received emotional support from rough draft thinking in my class. I loved this idea from one of my students: "Rough drafts can help encourage collaboration and trying even though you might doubt yourself." It's normal to doubt ourselves, but we all need support to try while experiencing self-doubt. I hope these future teachers give their students chances to talk through their thinking and to be emotionally supported while doing so.

To encourage my students to connect their experiences as learners with their futures as teachers, I asked them to write an end-of-the-semester reflection essay assignment in response to an open prompt: *Think back on your experience in the course this semester. Explain how specific ideas about teaching impacted your learning. Describe ways in which these ideas will become part of your own teaching practice once you get into a classroom.*

In these reflections, I was relieved that the prospective teachers noticed some of my instructional choices around promoting rough draft thinking, because I assumed that I didn't talk about my teaching moves explicitly enough during class. They recognized specific ways I attempted to create a safe space for sharing their mathematical thinking and opportunities to revise their thinking.

> Whenever one of the students was demonstrating problems on the overhead, Dr. Jansen wanted us to comment on what we thought was good, what we liked, what we agreed with, and so forth. She had a few examples on the board of little phrases that would help us start a classroom discussion or conversation. She had multiple phrases, some of which included, "I agree with," "I resonate with," "I like what you did here," "I don't quite understand," and some others. This really made me comfortable with talking to everyone in the class and didn't make me afraid to ask questions when I was confused. This made me think that in my classroom in the future I might do the same thing. I thought about having a set of beginning phrases that my kids could use to ask me

> questions. Some kids are scared to ask questions or don't know how to approach a question and I think that this really could motivate them to speak up and voice their concerns.
>
> —Preservice elementary teacher

I appreciated that this prospective teacher made the connection between engaging in discourse to make sense of one another's thinking and feeling emotionally safe to participate during class. Sentence starters can validate that it's okay and appropriate to wonder about another person's thinking or appreciate a peer's work.

> Another way that this class was taught that will help me with my teaching in the future is having kids try a problem first and then have them "revise their thinking." Having kids brainstorm and mess around with ideas gets them thinking in multiple different ways. Every kid doesn't learn exactly the same, so if they find a way that works better for them they can use that. However, if a student makes a mistake or gets stuck once they've tried it, I can then direct them in the right direction, and it'll make more sense to them. Something else that I think goes along with "revising your thinking" is having kids work in groups so that they see how other people think. One way that a kid might think of something is not the same way another kid might think of the same exact topic. This could be demonstrated on an overhead projector, and the teacher could say to the class, "Here class, (Name) has started this problem, but doesn't quite understand where to go from here, who could help (Name) out." Kids then feel empowered that they're helping one of their classmates out and are telling aloud to the class their way of thinking."
>
> —Preservice elementary teacher

I appreciated that this prospective teacher experienced doing math as a process of brainstorming and "messing around," because exploratory thinking opens us up to making new connections. I was glad to read that this student noticed that I had class members share their initial ideas, even when they weren't sure. Building on the initial starting points can be a helpful way to mathematically move forward together on the problem as a class.

> One of the biggest things that impacted me in this course as a future educator was the thought process behind "rough drafts" in math. We started out almost every single class using whiteboards to demonstrate our thinking in some kind of warm-up problem. I thought this was a unique idea. This allowed students to fix their mistakes without having to erase the whole thing simply because we were using a whiteboard. This also allowed students to display their work and share it with other students because they were large whiteboards. Almost every single problem we discussed in class, a student was asked to share their thoughts about it out loud. Or they might have been asked to come up to the front and explain how they found their answer. If a student was struggling, that student was asked to express their current thoughts about the problem, given encouragement, and then given support from classmates to further their thinking and eventually solve the problem.
>
> —Preservice elementary teacher

Whiteboards seem to go well with rough draft thinking, so I was glad to have a classroom set. I've often been curious as to why students find whiteboards to be so freeing. On a nonpermanent surface, I suppose that students do not feel pressured to write down ideas with certainty. This is interesting to me, because pencils are also not permanent. Perhaps writing on paper might feel more permanent? Maybe this is because dry erase boards are usually erased completely, and what we write on paper often remains there. We only erase what we need to fix or change on paper. Writing on a whiteboard must feel like less of a commitment.

Peter Liljedahl (2016) explored this idea in his work. He studied students' experiences in high school classrooms. Students working in groups were more eager to start problems, quicker to discuss, more persistent, and more likely to work nonlinearly when they worked on whiteboards compared to using paper. Students took more risks often and quickly when they could erase easily. The risks involved with sharing early drafts appear to be reduced when students use whiteboards.

I was also pleased that this prospective teacher realized that I would encourage students to share when they were unsure. It is true that I find value in hearing people's current thoughts about what they're doing. I made this explicit with my students by asking, *How are you currently thinking about this problem?* It feels like a liberating question, because it emphasizes that our thinking is evolving. It prevents freezing people in time. If we don't fully understand right now, that doesn't mean that we won't have a deeper understanding later.

> Creating rough drafts of our work and sharing different ideas with our groups allowed for me to view problems in various ways that were unfamiliar. This ultimately deepened my understanding of the concepts we were discussing in class because I was working to find the solution from multiple points of thought. Having the opportunity to complete a problem in an unfamiliar format really allowed for me to know whether or not I understood the material entirely. Additionally, having myself and classmates show our thinking on the projector and going through each step individually was a helpful method that impacted my learning in this course. Besides being able to see another person's thought process, it allowed me to hear explanations from different people, which can be more helpful than listening to the same person explain something over and over. It also required me to explain my own thinking in a way that others could understand, which helped me grasp a fuller understanding of the material. Having the option to make quiz corrections was not only beneficial to my grade, but it also gave me the opportunity to see where my understanding is not complete. Revising my work had me rethink about the problem and the concepts I needed to work on. This not only had me reflect on previous ideas discussed in class but allowed me to better prepare for the upcoming exam because I was aware of what skills I needed to work on.
>
> —Preservice elementary teacher

Like other students, this prospective teacher experienced that sharing thinking and listening to peers' thinking invited ways to move forward and learn more. This student also highlighted my quiz revision practice. This course had three quizzes and three exams. I did not allow opportunities to revise exams, but I did allow opportunities to revise quizzes.

> Another concept that we used during this class that I found very useful was revising your own thinking. I liked that it was okay to be wrong in this class and that your classmates would not judge you for it but would instead help you to see where you had gone wrong in your thinking or in your arithmetic. I think that having rough drafts in math is extremely beneficial and can be very helpful when teaching new concepts. Teaching kids that they need to understand new concepts immediately can be harmful to their self-esteem and to their motivation if they do not grasp concepts right away. I think that sharing incomplete solutions and being able to use classmates' ideas to complete your own work creates a community of open communication that can help with understanding.
>
> —Preservice elementary teacher

I was delighted to read that this prospective teacher reflected that learners may "not grasp concepts right away." Learning anything new takes a great deal of time and effort (including, apparently, learning to enact teaching to promote rough draft thinking). I want to create a "community of open communication," but I do not recall using that phrase in class. I am glad that this student experienced such a community in my course this semester.

Naming and Labeling my Instructional Choices

After I read my prospective teachers' responses and reflections, I decided to cut myself some slack. Before I read their thoughts, I assumed I hadn't done enough. I could have given the prospective teachers more explicit revision opportunities. I assumed I hadn't talked about my own instructional decision-making enough for the prospective teachers to have concrete ideas about the value of rough draft thinking and how to promote it in their classrooms. I realized after checking in with my students, however, that I supported them more than I realized. I don't have to enact everything I want to try to make a difference. To help my students experience a spirit of rough draft thinking about *learning* mathematics, it seems useful for me to have a spirit of rough draft thinking about my *teaching* of mathematics.

So, what did I do and how often did I do it? I sat down to summarize the steps I took to implement rough draft thinking during this particular semester.

MANDY'S IMPLEMENTATION OF ROUGH DRAFT THINKING

Launching the Course

- Seek out students' incoming perspectives related to rough draft thinking
- Be explicit with students about how learning takes place
- Get to know students
- Visibly random grouping daily

Managing Discussions and Implementing Tasks: Centering Students' Thinking

- Strategically select work to be shared with goals for revision in mind
- Students revise their work at the document camera
- Display strategically selected work anonymously
- Encourage nonevaluative discourse so that students seek to understand one another
- Respond to students' thinking with curiosity

Looking back, I can see that I layered in some instructional choices that promoted a classroom culture of rough draft thinking, including how I implemented tasks. I did not have students explicitly revise their work as often as I intended. It turned out that I did "it"—rough draft thinking—both more and less than I thought I would when teaching my own math class.

My goal in fostering a culture of rough draft thinking was to help future teachers see that talking through ideas helps us develop our mathematical understandings together. I hoped they would come to see understanding as something that develops incrementally and evolves constantly. I wanted students to view our mathematics classwork as drafts that we continually revise, even when the drafts are technically "correct."

Launching the Course

I wanted to start the course off well by getting to know my students and being direct with them about my beliefs about learning. As I wrote earlier in the chapter, I asked my students what they thought about rough draft thinking before the semester started. This exercise allowed me both to foreshadow an idea I valued and to understand their thinking before meeting them. I've experimented with different prompts to get to know my students' incoming ideas related to rough draft thinking, and these are some that I have used recently on a Google Form that I distributed before the first day of classes.

I first asked my students to respond to a multiple-choice item, modified from open-ended items written for my previous efforts to study rough draft thinking in a mathematics content course for teachers (Thanheiser and Jansen 2016).

During mathematics class discussions, I...

- ○ **am willing to share my ideas out loud to the class whether or not I am sure I am correct.**
- ○ **will not share my ideas out loud to the class unless I am sure I am correct.**
- ○ **do not want to share my ideas out loud to the class at all.**

I like this item because it aligns with my goals for my classroom culture. I want students to feel as if it's fine to share their ideas at any stage. I worry that it's obvious that there is a "right" answer to this question and that students will answer in the ways that they think I want them to answer rather than telling me the truth. However, I have asked a version of this question quite often in interviews and surveys, and I do get a wide range of responses.

Alternatively, the open-ended item could be administered in a follow-up survey, maybe as an exit ticket:

Think about a time when you shared your thinking during mathematics class and it wasn't quite correct or fully worked out. What happened? How did you feel?

When I have posed this question in the past, some students say that it was helpful because they were able to make sense out of their thinking and learn more. Some people said that it had no impact on them either way. Others said that it was embarrassing and devastating. Responses to this question often reveal how their previous teachers handled these sorts of situations. Their responses also tell me whether they will enter my class with a view of talking-to-learn, which aligns well with rough draft talk, or talking-to-perform.

I was explicit with my students about my own beliefs about how learning takes place. I wanted to create a culture of talking-to-learn. I told my students directly about my beliefs about learning at the beginning of the semester and periodically reminded them throughout the semester. I posted Rights of the Learner on a slide and discussed them (see Chapter 2). I also required my students to watch a YouCubed (2016) video about how mistakes help your brain make new connections. Although I do not think that telling students what I believe is enough to change their beliefs, it seems better to be explicit with students.

★ Get to Know Students

I continued my effort to get to know students early in the semester in the first few weeks of class. I used Sara VanDerWerf's (2016a) idea of name tents with feedback, on which students wrote a comment or question to me at the end of every class for the first five class periods, and I wrote back to them (2016a). I provided the students with this prompt for the name tents:

Communicate with Mandy! Write a comment OR question OR make a suggestion about this class (ideally a couple of sentences). Each day I will respond to whatever you write. Leave this name tent on your table each day.

POSSIBLE QUESTIONS TO RESPOND TO:

How do you feel about math?

What would you like me to know about you outside of school?

What hopes do you have for this class?

How are you feeling about what we are learning about right now?

What do you like about math or this class?

What are you fearful of?

What activities (sports/arts/jobs) are you involved in after school?

Draw a picture/sketch of how you are feeling.

Draw a picture/sketch of something that represents you.

I found it useful to give prompts for the name tent feedback forms, because students were not used to being asked to write anything they wanted to their professor. The prompts helped the students see that I was truly open to reading whatever they wanted to share.

I also got to know my students by requiring them to sign up for in-person meetings in my office during the first couple of weeks of the semester. I blocked off extra office hours and students signed up for times that fit their schedules. The meetings were about thirty minutes long. About three or four students participated together in each meeting. In these meetings, I would ask my students to tell me and one another why they decided to become a teacher, as all of the students in the course were seeking an elementary education certification. I also asked them to share some significant memories doing mathematics in elementary school and to compare how these experiences were similar to or different from doing mathematics in my class. This could be a good question to have with one-on-one or group meetings with students of any age:

What are some of your significant memories of doing mathematics in earlier grades? How are these experiences similar to or different from doing mathematics in my class?

The students tended to share traumas from their pasts related to speed and fluency, such as timed tests, as well as moments of pride or of understanding. When comparing their past experiences to my current course, it was a good opportunity for me to highlight my intentions and goals for the class in terms of developing a value for rough draft thinking.

Thinking back to when I taught middle school, it would not have been realistic for me to have meetings with every student within a short period of time. I had too many students and not enough time for "office hours." But I have thought about what I could have realistically tried to do to build relationships with my students.

Relationships could be built through writing. I could invite students to journal entries to me about their stories as mathematics learners, using the same prompt. I could do this one class period at a time, which could give me time to write back to each student. It could be an ongoing process. The correspondence would not be for a grade. We would write for the value of interaction and knowing one another. It would be like a modified version of a mathematical autobiography to inspire dialogue.

★ Visibly Random Grouping Daily

Almost every single day, I determined where students sat by randomly distributing their name tents into groups of four students at a table. I kept doing this well after I learned students' names. They patiently waited for me to distribute the name tents before the start of class, which I did visibly, in front of them, so they could see groupings really were random.

I told students my rationale for visibly random grouping, building again on the work of Peter Liljedahl (2014). I posted and talked about a slide with this information on the first day of classes:

> . . . the use of *visibly random grouping* strategies, along with ubiquitous group work, can lead to:

1. students becoming agreeable to work in any group they are placed in
2. the elimination of social barriers within the classroom
3. an increase in the mobility of knowledge between students
4. a decrease in reliance on the teacher for answers
5. an increase in the reliance on co-constructed intra- and intergroup answers
6. an increase in both enthusiasm for mathematics class and engagement in mathematics tasks.

In their end-of-the-semester reflection, a few students returned to this experience of random grouping and mentioned its value.

One student wrote:

> One of the teaching techniques that I learned was that mixing up the seating arrangement every class to ensure that students get to think about things differently and collaborate with different people. Switching seats for every class period was really cool because by the end of the semester we all were like a family. There were some people in that class that I never thought would be interested in being friends with me became my friends and some of my colleagues [from this class] sat with me in other classes which was cool. Moving the students' seats around can help them get to know everyone and also gives them new perspectives and ways of thinking.
>
> —Preservice elementary teacher

A second student wrote:

> Another idea from class this semester that really stood out to me was the rotating seating . . . each person sat at a new place every time the class met. This was a really positive experience for me because it allowed me to become familiar with my classmates quite fast. In another class, I may have known everyone's face, but not their name, and I definitely would not have spoken to everyone at least once during my time in the class. Just like the aforementioned open sharing atmosphere, this rotating seating arrangement helps me to become comfortable with my classmates and helps me know that I can talk to them about the material no matter what. For someone like me, who is quite shy and introverted around people whom I don't know, this was a good method to force me out of my shell and actively communicate with my classmates. I think this is a good strategy to use with kids of all ages, as it teaches good teamwork and communication skills. I would definitely use this in my classroom to enforce a collaborative and friendly environment that actively facilitates learning for any subject—not just mathematics.
>
> —Preservice elementary teacher

I was so pleased that these students felt seen and heard by their classmates as a result of the random seating. Both of these students appeared to be rather quiet students. They had to be nudged to share their thinking aloud in front of the entire class. It is interesting to me that these two students thought to comment on how much they valued the random seating arrangements on a daily basis.

Managing Discussions and Implementing Tasks: Centering Students' Thinking

As an instructor of a course that had multiple sections, with different sections taught by other instructors, I did not have control over which tasks my students were assigned. The instructors taught out of common lesson plans. Students solved the same problems during class and for homework across all sections. However, I did have autonomy as an instructor over how I managed discussions when implementing tasks.

When I spend time in high schools and middle schools, I wish I could see students up at the front of the room more often. I reflected that, if I want to see students at the front of the room in other teachers' classrooms, I need to make sure I do this myself in my own classroom. This is particularly important because my students are future teachers, and I'm modeling instructional practice for them. I made it my goal for every class session to have multiple students share their work at the document camera when we reviewed homework and debriefed from group work.

One thing I am most proud of from this semester is that I think I did a better job than I normally do strategically selecting students' work to be shared and discussed at the document camera (Smith and Sherin 2019). I found it useful to develop criteria for selecting work based on promoting rough draft thinking. I wanted students to develop a perspective that mathematical thinking could constantly be revised and that their work could be shared at any stage.

★ Strategically Select Work to Be Shared with Goals for Revision in Mind

At the start of the semester, if I did not strategically select students' work when I asked students to share at the document camera, I noticed that my students were not sure how to comment on one another's thinking. A student would describe their thinking. I would then ask the class what they thought about the work. Students would stare back at me. I realized that I was choosing student work to be displayed without a goal for what I wanted my students to consider about the work.

So, to prepare to teach, I would work on the problems for that day's lesson and set goals for revision by anticipating ways of thinking that students would be more and less likely to enact, as well as common errors. Then, when implementing the task, I strategically selected a range of answers or solutions for a single problem, both correct and incorrect, to be displayed to the class.

In thinking about how to select students' work for whole-class discussions, I decided to focus on the potential for revision in the work (Table 6.2). If I selected students' work carefully, the class could collectively refine it. As I walked around and looked at students' work, I would ask myself, *How could this work be improved through the class discussion?* Incomplete and incorrect work could clearly be revised, but what about correct work?

Correct work could have more illuminating representations, an explanation could become more concise or include alternative word choices, or maybe it could be elaborated on further. It was important to me that I communicated to students that work that appeared fine and correct on the surface could still be improved.

SELECTING STUDENTS' WORK FOR DISCUSSION WITH REVISING IN MIND

Criteria for Selecting Student Work	Opportunity for Revision	Questions About the Work (First ask the student to talk about their thinking and to explain their work.)
Correct explanations	Could be improved through better clarity, more visuals, more detail.	What more do we need to have written down for someone else to make sense of this solution? Imagine if someone was absent today. What would that person need to see written down to understand your thinking? How could you use that lens to improve your explanation?
Incomplete solutions	Could be improved through being finished.	What do you think they would do next? Why? How does this way of getting started on the problem provide inspiration for you in your work on this problem?
Incorrect solutions	Could be improved by being corrected.	What makes sense to you about how they were thinking? What questions do you have about their thinking? Did you do anything differently? What? Why did you do it this way?

TABLE 6.2

I had a goal of working with students to refine work that looked correct. It's so prevalent to think about mathematics as either correct or incorrect, and I wanted to challenge that perception. One approach has been to work toward clearer communication in the written solution. The answer might be there, but the process or justification behind the answer might be difficult to follow as written. The class could collectively revise the student's work so that the explanation is clearly articulated.

When I asked students to share incomplete solutions, students have shared privately that they felt validated. They would worry that they were the only one who did not fully understand. Seeing that another person was also stuck gave them some relief. An incomplete solution helped me amplify that we can appreciate what we do understand so far. Then, the group can push forward to work together to complete the explanation.

Selecting and sequencing students' thinking is an important part of leading a classroom discussion (Smith and Stein 2019). It was powerful for me to realize that I could use the idea of revision as a way to choose which students should share their work.

★ Students Revise Their Work at the Document Camera

When students came to the document camera to explain their thinking, I tried to consistently communicate they were sharing early drafts. I let students know that I expected their work to continue to evolve while sharing and discussing it. Students would realize through explaining to the class that their written work did not yet have enough clarity. Students' work would be written in pencil, and I had markers available at the document camera. While explaining to the class, students would annotate their work and revise in the moment.

For example, in our proportional reasoning unit, we worked on this problem:

> Olivia picked out 8 posters that cost a total of $10. On her way to the checkout counter, she decided that she really wanted 12 posters. If all of the posters were the same price, how much would she pay for 12 posters?
>
> - Steven thinks she will pay $14.
> - Joey thinks she will pay $15.
>
> Explain how each person came up with their answer.
> Who is correct? Why?

This problem was designed with the assumption that some students might initially use additive reasoning rather than multiplicative reasoning to determine the final cost. There are many ways to solve the task:

- Unit rate ($1.25 per poster)
- Scale factor within units (Olivia wanted to buy 1.5 times as many posters as she initially thought she would buy, so she paid 1.5 times as much.)
- Scale factor across units (10 is 1 and $\frac{1}{4}$ times as much as 8, so she's paying 1.25 times as much as the number of posters she purchased.)
- Scaling up and down (8 posters for $10 is similar to 4 posters for $5, so we can combine these equivalent ratios to find how much 12 posters would cost.)

I assumed students would use unit rate, so I chose a student to present who used a different strategy.

Allison presented that 8 times 1.5 is 12, so 10 times 1.5 is $15. This meant that the answer was $15. When presenting, the class had questions for how to find the scale factor. Allison then used a marker to write out her strategy for finding the scale factor in greater detail. Within 12 was one full group of 8, with 4 left. Four is half of 8, so one-and-a-half groups of 8 are in 12. So, we need one-and-a-half groups of $10 for the new price that Olivia is paying. In this way, Allison's revision was an elaboration of reasoning underlying her solution.

During the discussion, I continued to elicit a range of strategies and highlighted connections between them. For instance, some students wrote out the following equivalent ratios to try to find the solution a second way:

8 posters for $10.00

4 posters for $5.00

2 posters for $2.50

1 poster for $1.25

12 × (1 poster for $1.25) = 12 posters for $15

Then they could illustrate that you could have found the solution by adding 8 posters and 4 posters to get 12 posters for $15, but if you multiplied 12 times 1 poster and 12 times $1.25, this was like scaling up and down to find the unit rate and then using the unit rate to find the answer. Another way to think about revising our (correct) thinking, then, was extending our thinking by connections between strategies during the discussion.

A student who made this connection, between scaling up and down with equivalent ratios and finding the unit rate, highlighted that connection with markers at the document camera. The student circled "1 poster for $1.25," and wrote *unit rate*. Then I asked if there would have been a way to find how much one poster cost without as many equivalent ratios. On the side, with the marker, the student then divided $10 by 8 posters. I highlighted that one solution is not better than another, because sometimes scaling with equivalent ratios can also be efficient. I wanted students to see how the solutions were related.

I used to have students stay at their seats when talking about their thinking. They would verbally explain their solutions. Maybe I would have recorded their thinking or maybe not. I find that I now prefer having students' verbal explanations recorded in writing, because it helps the class follow along and their thinking is preserved. I prefer having the student record their own solutions, so they can decide how their thinking should be represented. Having the student in the front of the room centers their ideas and having them record their thinking in writing complements the oral description of the solution.

What's been interesting to me is that simply having markers available at the document camera has invited revision in the moment. Because we refine our thinking as we talk, students want to add to what they already wrote down as they explain their work. I like having different colors of writing instruments, not just another pencil, because then we can see which ideas were generated during the whole-group sharing time.

★ Display Strategically Selected Work Anonymously

One implementation strategy I used less often was to display students' work anonymously rather than having a student go up to the document camera. If a student had work that I thought the class would benefit from discussing, but the student was hesitant to participate, their work could be one of the solutions shared anonymously. Maybe if they experienced the class interacting around their work when it is anonymously displayed, they might feel more comfortable sharing their work publicly in the future.

As an example, consider a task with multiple possible correct answers. We introduced our proportional reasoning unit by having the students create equivalent ratios.

> Imagine a bag with 15 blue marbles and 5 red marbles.
>
> What are some combinations of marbles that could be created to have bags of similar groupings of marbles?

I anticipated that students would be more likely to create larger quantities of marbles rather than fewer. I thought I would see 30 blue and 10 red, 300 blue and 100 red, 60 blue and 20 red, and so forth. I then circulated the room to look for some smaller quantities, like 3 blue and 1 red, 6 blue and 2 red, 9 blue and 3 red, and so on.

I also anticipated that the ratios from students would tend to be multiples of 15 and 5, such as 45 blue and 15 red. I assumed that ratios like 12 blue and 4 red would not be found by most of the students. We could emphasize that once we have ratio with one of the values as 1 (3 blue and 1 red), this ratio could be used for finding more equivalent ratios.

I collected a range of correct answers and shared them anonymously to spark discussion. I hoped to push students to find new ways to see other correct ratios. Again, when implementing tasks, it was important for me to emphasize that correct ways of thinking could still be refined and extended.

I conjecture that anonymous sharing has a lot of benefits. Anonymous sharing can keep the focus on the ideas and off of the people who generated the ideas. For students who don't identify as extroverted, their work can still be shared and appreciated in ways that allow them to be themselves. If a student is hesitant to share, this is a way for their work to be public to support others' learning.

★ Encourage Nonevaluative Discourse so that Students Seek to Understand One Another

I wondered what my students thought about the purpose of sharing their thinking in mathematics class, and if they thought that the purpose was to learn from one another. It was my responsibility to create an intellectual need to talk about one another's work, and perhaps I hadn't done that yet. I conjectured that some of my students primarily thought that it was important to listen to me when I spoke. I wondered whether they thought that they were being evaluated by me when they were speaking in front of the class. That is an understandable perspective if they had been students for many years in classrooms where those perspectives were in place. It was my job to help my students understand that I was asking them to share their thinking because they have something to learn from one another, not just from me.

I wanted students to use nonevaluative discourse so that they would focus on making sense of one another's thinking, including what helped them learn something new. I decided that they needed support to do this. I displayed sentence starters so that students would have inspiration for how they could begin to talk about a peer's solution. I chose sentence starters that promoted making sense of another person's ideas. My students tended to pick up and use these sentence starters more than others:

- That makes sense to me because . . .
- I agree because . . .
- I don't know what you mean by . . .
- I also did that because . . .

I didn't have to display the sentence starters every day for the students to internalize and use them. I only publicly displayed sentence starters (see the full list in Chapter 2) for three class sessions at the most, but they seemed to make a difference. The essential aspect of these sentence starters was that they helped students access ways of talking about their peers' thinking that emphasized trying to understand, not evaluate one another.

My go-to questions that seemed to help students engage in making sense of their peers' work were as follows: *What do you notice? What are you wondering about? What do you appreciate?* After students shared their work on the document camera, I would channel the power of noticing and wondering (Fetter 2011; Ray-Riek 2013). I was surprised that asking students to notice and wonder about their peers' work did not get old. If I didn't know what else to ask the class after students shared their work at the document camera, I would turn to the class and ask these questions, and they elicited multiple responses.

When students did not have many comments about work from a peer displayed at the document camera, I explicitly told them that I believed that they had something to learn from their peers' solutions. They were studying to become future teachers, so I asserted that it was helpful to listen to other people's mathematical thinking and try to understand it, because teachers constantly need to try to understand their students' mathematical thinking. They could start to do this by trying to understand the mathematical thinking of their peers.

I also shared that I did not see mathematics classrooms as a place where the teacher imparts knowledge to students. Instead, they are a community where a group of people work together to build their mathematical understanding. Everyone continues to learn, including the teacher. To build understanding, we have to be willing to individually try to understand, share our current understandings, and try to make sense of what our colleagues currently understand. Then we can revisit our own ideas based on what we heard a colleague share.

★ Respond to Students' Thinking with Curiosity

When I implemented tasks, I became more aware of how I responded to students' thinking. My first efforts were focused on being neutral. I didn't want to get excited only about correct answers. I wanted to value incorrect thinking as well as correct thinking. But then I started to be afraid that neutral was coming across as indifferent, so I decided to model genuine curiosity about everyone's thinking, in hopes that students would see my curiosity as valuing thinking and pick up that practice themselves. I thought it was important to notice something of value in students' thinking in a nonevaluative way. I would say, "Tell us more about how you . . ." or "What inspired you to get started this way?" I would get excited about all of the ways of thinking I hadn't tried myself, and there were always examples to find. Modeling my own evolution in thinking about mathematics during our class discussions seemed to rehumanize the learning experience, because I would exclaim how I hadn't thought about it that way or I would admit that I first got stuck at that point of the problem as well.

Explicit Revision Opportunities

I have mentioned that I thought I did not offer enough explicit revision opportunities for students, but on reflection, I realized that I did incorporate some revision experiences. I primarily relied on inspiration from the Stronger and Clearer Each Time routine described in Chapter 4 as I taught this course. To help students make sense of mathematical vocabulary concepts, I asked students to write definitions in their own words, trade their definitions and read a classmate's definition, and then write a stronger and clearer definition inspired by their classmate's definition. I also allowed students to revise their quizzes in this course.

Stronger and Clearer Each Time

Because this course was about rational number concepts, I implemented the Stronger and Clearer Each Time routine to foster sense-making about "numerator" and "denominator." I expected that students would define *denominator* as the number of times the whole is equally partitioned (or split up). That would determine the relative size of a unit fraction as being larger or smaller (e.g., $\frac{1}{12}$ is smaller than $\frac{1}{5}$ because when you take the same whole and equally partition it more times, each piece is smaller). I expected that students would define *numerator* as the number of pieces of the unit fraction included in the quantity. These definitions, or some similar set of ideas, would be consistent with how I had been talking with the class: the numerator representing the number of pieces and the denominator representing the size of a piece in a fraction.

Each student had a blank page to complete that looked like Table 6.3:

MANDY'S TEMPLATE FOR STRONGER AND CLEARER EACH TIME

	numerator	denominator
First draft		
Second draft		

TABLE 6.3

Scott and Allison were partners, and their initial drafts for numerator and denominator are displayed in Table 6.4.

SCOTT'S AND ALLISON'S FIRST DRAFT DEFINITIONS

	numerator	denominator
Scott's first draft	The digit on the top half of a fraction represents a portion of a whole	Digit on bottom half of a fraction, represents a whole
Allison's first draft	Top number, number of pieces, quantity	Bottom number, size of each piece, defining size of quantity

TABLE 6.4

Then I asked them to trade their definitions with each other. They read and discussed their definitions. Their second drafts were expected to be informed by their classmate's definitions, as seen in Table 6.5.

SCOTT'S AND ALLISON'S SECOND DRAFT DEFINITIONS

	numerator	denominator
Scott's second draft	Tells how many pieces of a whole	Defines size of quantity
Allison's second draft	Top number in the fraction, which is how many parts of a whole we have, or the quantity	Bottom number in the fraction, which represents how many parts make a whole and defines the size of the quantity

TABLE 6.5

Scott moved away from describing location (top and bottom number) in his second draft to focus on quantitative relationships, as informed by Allison's first draft. Allison's second draft added in these location features that Scott had described.

An important orientation for learners during a Stronger and Clearer Each Time routine is assuming that we can learn from any of our colleagues. Allison reflected that she originally did not mention the whole in her definition of numerator, and she changed her definition to include this idea. It can be useful to ask students how they changed their definitions and what inspired the changes.

An important orientation for teachers during a Stronger and Clearer Each Time routine is not to expect revised definitions to be fully complete or correct. This process is a formative assessment activity. We get access to how our students are currently thinking. Their revised definitions could be improved, or they could be slightly less strong after revising. Whatever the students write serves as insight about how they currently think about the concepts.

I also implemented a simpler version of Stronger and Clearer Each Time using whiteboards. I asked students to take their individual whiteboards and solve a problem. Then, I had them trade whiteboards with their partner and review their classmate's strategies. I invited them to discuss strategies with one another. When students took their original whiteboards back, they revised their work based on inspiration from their classmate.

Quiz Revisions

As mentioned previously in this chapter, I also allowed students to revise their quizzes, but students did not revise their exams. This course had three exams and three quizzes. Quizzes were not worth as many points as exams, so the revisions did not result in dramatic changes to their overall course grade. Students appreciated opportunities to revise some of their assessments.

I gave students this protocol for revising their quizzes: For each problem that did not receive full credit, they could earn all of the points back if their revisions included responses to these prompts:

1. **How could your solution be improved, and why would the changes be improvements?**
2. **Write up a full and complete new solution in response to the original quiz question.**

It was important for me to read students' reflections about why the revision was better than the original, in part because they could have copied a peer's correct solution, but primarily because reflection leads to continued learning (Boud, Keogh, and Walker 2013).

I wonder whether I should allow students to revise or retake exams as well as quizzes. Revising quizzes and not exams was a compromise made to accommodate the instructors who did not want any assessments revised. Giving an exam without an opportunity to revise freezes thinking at a particular point in time and privileges that performance with an evaluation. But learning hopefully continues. I wonder whether or how I can give students more chances to show how their thinking evolves. For now, having a cumulative final exam that is worth more points than the other two exams somewhat serves the purpose that a retake or revision of an exam might serve.

Moving Forward

So, how often did I do it? If the "it" in rough draft thinking is asking students to revise their thinking in an explicit way, I only implemented

Stronger and Clearer Each Time a couple of times during the semester. Also, there were only three quizzes to revise. I conjecture that the classroom culture efforts to support practices for making sense of mathematics and for making sense of one another's mathematics were more important, but they were also more subtle.

I was sincerely surprised that my students had so much to say when I asked them to share what they thought about rough draft thinking at the end of the semester. I thought that because I didn't facilitate enough explicit revision experiences with them, they wouldn't have a strong response to my question. I thought I hadn't done enough.

As I wrote this chapter, I was surprised by the efforts I was able to name and label. This reflection helped me to see that I did more to promote rough draft thinking than I remembered doing. That's a good lesson about reflecting on my own practice: To realize the strengths in my work, I benefit from slowing down, recording my instructional choices, and writing about why I made them. I can also ask my students how things are going, and I might find that the class is unfolding better than I assumed.

That said, every time I teach the course again, I want to include more explicit revision experiences. I can use the Stronger and Clearer Each Time routine in other ways, such as for explaining which fraction is larger than another or for justifying why the multiplication algorithm for fractions makes sense, so students can continue to crystallize their thinking and learning. I will make a list of course goals and schedule more Stronger and Clearer Each Time activities into the course.

I also have ideas to continue to foster my classroom culture. I have recently been sitting in students' seats when they are at the document camera, and that option has been beneficial for fostering student-to-student discourse. Previously, I noticed that I tended to stand near students and hover at the document camera near them, which led to me jumping into their explanations sometimes. If I remove myself physically from the front of the room, I reduce my role as authority and hopefully transfer more authority to my students.

I also started keeping a better record of which students come up to the document camera and for what reasons. I bought a clipboard and printed out a class list. I am starting to develop a coding system to use in real time to document participation. Some of the codes are Commented (upon a colleague's solution or noticed something), Asked (a question or posed a wonderment), Selected (by me to share work at the document camera), and Volunteered (a willingness to share their own work at the document camera). Before the next class, I review who the class has heard from recently, and I highlight the names of students whose voices haven't been heard. That way I can consider strategically selecting their thinking to be shared at the document camera if their work also aligns with my goals for the lesson.

In addition, I have brainstormed revisions to my list of sentence starters to help students focus on appreciating one another's thinking. I'd like my students to shift from evaluating one another's thinking to seeking to understand one another, toward appreciating what their peers have to offer. Some sentence starters that focus on appreciation include "I learned from you when you . . ." "What you said about ______________ helped me see things in a new way because . . ."

It has been helpful to view my teaching as a draft in itself. It is useful to find strengths in early drafts rather than focusing on what did not happen. If I view my teaching as a work in progress, I can build on the strengths as I push myself to continue to grow.

I want to end this chapter by going back to Carla, the coach from the beginning of the chapter who asked me how often her teachers should do rough draft math. After our conversation, I asked Carla about how she started to work with her teachers on rough draft thinking. She decided to work with a fifth-grade teacher on incorporating a Round of Rough Draft Sharing. Students began working on a challenging task, the *Bobsled Sums* problem (National Council of Teachers of Mathematics 2018), as a problem of the week. After spending time working on the problem, but not enough time to finish it, the teacher asked the students to share how they got started on the problem. Students shared their initial attempts for solving it at the document camera for a Round of Rough Draft Sharing. After trying the Round of Rough Draft Sharing with a fifth-grade teacher, Carla tweeted:

> Scholars sharing different strategies they used to begin solving a POW [Problem of the Week] word problem. The conversations were amazing and provided an entry point for some who were hesitant to begin.

For Carla and her colleagues, a helpful way to get started with rough draft thinking was with this Round of Rough Draft Sharing.

There are many ways to get started with inviting rough draft thinking, just like there are many ways to get started on a challenging mathematical task. There is no one best approach, and there is no single right way to do it. As long as we're inviting students to see that their rough drafts help them and their classmates learn, and as long as we give students spaces to continually improve their thinking, we're well on our way to supporting our students through incorporating rough draft thinking. To honor our efforts to improve our practice, it helps to treat ourselves as works in progress.

I look forward to continuing to learn more from teachers who share with me how they engage their students in rough draft thinking during mathematics class. For anyone who wants to share their thinking in response to this book, please use the hashtag #RoughDraftMath on Twitter. I'm @MandyMathEd. I hope to hear from you!

REFERENCES

Aguirre, J., K. Mayfield-Ingram, and D. Martin. 2013. *The Impact of Identity in K–8 Mathematics: Rethinking Equity-Based Practices.* Reston, VA: National Council of Teachers of Mathematics.

Ames, C. 1992. "Classrooms: Goals, Structures, and Student Motivation." *Journal of Educational Psychology* 84 (3): 261–271.

Anghileri, J. 2006. "Scaffolding Practices That Enhance Mathematics Learning." *Journal of Mathematics Teacher Education* 9:33–52.

Barnes, D. 2008. "Exploratory Talk for Learning." In *Exploring Talk in School: Inspired by the Work of Douglas Barnes*, ed. N. Mercer and S. Hodgkinson (pp. 1–15). London: Sage.

Boud, D., R. Keogh, and D. Walker. 2013. *Reflection: Turning Experience into Learning*. London: Routledge.

Brantlinger, A. 2018. "Humanizing and Dehumanizing Trends in a Critical Math Classroom." In *Inside the Mathematics Class: Sociological Perspectives on Participation, Inclusion, and Enhancement*, ed. C. Knipping, H. Straehler-Pohl, and U. Gellert (pp. 247–268). Cham, Switzerland: Springer.

Brown, S. I., and M. I. Walter. 1983. *The Art of Problem Posing*. Philadelphia: Franklin Institute Press.

Chapin, S. H., C. O'Connor, and N. C. Anderson. 2003. "Tools of Classroom Talk." In *Classroom Discussions: Using Math Talk to Help Students Learn* (pp. 12–42). Sausalito, CA: Math Solutions Publications.

Cohen, E. G., and R. A. Lotan. 1997. *Working for Equity in Heterogeneous Classrooms: Sociological Theory in Practice*. New York: Teachers College Press.

———. 2014. *Designing Group Work: Strategies for the Heterogeneous Classroom*. 3rd ed. New York: Teachers College Press.

Davis, B. 1997. "Listening for Differences: An Evolving Conception of Mathematics Teaching." *Journal for Research in Mathematics Education* 28 (3): 355–376.

Dawes, L. 2012. *Talking Points: Discussion Activities in the Primary Classroom*. New York: Routledge.

Dewey, J. 1968. *The School and Society.* Chicago: University of Chicago Press. Originally published in 1900.

Dick, L., T. F. White, A. Trocki, P. Sztajn, D. Heck, and K. Herrema. 2016. "Supporting Sense Making with Mathematical Bet Lines." *Teaching Children Mathematics* 22 (9): 538–545.

Dweck, C. S., and E. L. Leggett. 1988. "A Social-Cognitive Approach to Motivation and Personality." *Psychological Review* 95 (2): 256–273.

Dysarz, K. 2018. "Checking In: Are Math Assignments Measuring Up?" *The Education Trust*. https://edtrust.org/resource/checking-in-are-math-assignments-measuring-up/.

Ericson, D. P. 1991. "Humanization, Democracy, and Political Education." *Studies in Philosophy and Education* 11 (1): 31–43.

Fetter, A. 2011. "Ever Wonder What They'd Notice?" YouTube video. https://www.youtube.com/watch?v=a-Fth6sOaRA.

Fraser, S., D. Fendel, and D. Resek. 2011. *Interactive Mathematics Program: The Diver Returns*, 2nd ed. (pp. 3–7). Emeryville, CA: Key Curriculum Press.

Freudenthal, H. 1991. *Revisiting Mathematics Education: China Lectures*. Dordrecht: Kluwer Academic.

Goffney, I. 2019. "From Oakland to Wakanda: Transforming Mathematics Classrooms to Become Equitable and Empowering Spaces for Black and Brown Students." Presentation given at the Teachers Development Group Leadership Seminar, West Linn, Oregon, February 28.

Gutiérrez, R. 2017. "Living Mathematx: Towards a Vision for the Future." *Philosophy of Mathematics Education Journal* 32 (1).

———. 2018. "Rehumanizing Mathematics: A Vision for the Future." YouTube video. https://youtu.be/D266LYIigS0.

Guzmán, L. D., and J. Craig, 2019. "The World in Your Pocket: Digital Media as Invitations for Transdisciplinary Inquiry in Mathematics Classrooms." *Occasional Paper Series*, 2019 (41): 6.

Harvard Graduate School of Education. 2011. "I Used to Think . . ., but Now I Think . . ." Visible Thinking. http://www.visiblethinkingpz.org/VisibleThinking_html_files/03_ThinkingRoutines/03c_Core_routines/UsedToThink/UsedToThink_Routine.htm.

Herbel-Eisenmann, B. A., and M. Cirillo, eds. 2009. *Promoting Purposeful Discourse: Teacher Research in Mathematics Classrooms*. Reston, VA: National Council of Teachers of Mathematics.

Herbel-Eisenmann, B. A., M. D. Steele, and M. Cirillo. 2013. "(Developing) Teacher Discourse Moves: A Framework for Professional Development." *Mathematics Teacher Educator* 1 (2): 181–196.

Hiebert, J., and T. P. Carpenter, T. P. 1992. "Learning and Teaching with Understanding." In *Handbook of Research on Mathematics Teaching and Learning*, ed. D. A. Grouws (pp. 65-98). New York: Macmillan.

Hintz, A., K. Tyson, and A. R. English. 2018. "Actualizing the Rights of the Learner: The Role of Pedagogical Listening." *Democracy & Education* 26 (2): 8.

Hintz, A. B. 2011. "Understanding Students' Experiences as Listeners During Mathematical Discussion." *Canadian Journal of Science, Mathematics, and Technology Education* 11 (3): 261–272.

Honoré, C. 2004. *In Praise of Slowness: Challenging the Cult of Speed*. San Francisco: HarperOne.

———. 2005. "In Praise of Slowness." TED video. https://www.ted.com/talks/carl_honore_praises_slowness.

Humphreys, C., and R. Parker. 2015. *Making Number Talks Matter: Developing Mathematical Practices and Deepening Understanding, Grades 4–10*. Portland, ME: Stenhouse.

Jansen, A. 2006. "Seventh Graders' Motivations for Participating in Two Discussion-Oriented Mathematics Classrooms." *Elementary School Journal* 106 (5): 409–428.

———. 2008. "An Investigation of Relationships Between Seventh-Grade Students' Beliefs and Their Participation During Mathematics Discussions in Two Classrooms." *Mathematical Thinking and Learning* 10 (1): 68–100.

———. 2009. "Prospective Elementary Teachers' Motivation to Participate in Whole-Class Discussions During Mathematics Content Courses for Teachers." *Educational Studies in Mathematics* 71 (2): 145–160.

———. 2012. "Developing Productive Dispositions During Small-Group Work in Two Sixth-Grade Mathematics Classrooms: Teachers' Facilitation Efforts and Students' Self-Reported Benefits." *Middle Grades Research Journal* 7 (1): 37–56.

Jansen, A., B. Cooper, S. Vascellaro, and P. Wandless. 2017. "Rough-Draft Talk in Mathematics Classrooms." *Mathematics Teaching in the Middle School* 22 (5): 304–307.

Jansen, A., B. Herbel-Eisenmann, and J. P. Smith III. 2012. "Detecting Students' Experiences of Discontinuities Between Middle School and High School Mathematics Programs: Learning During Boundary Crossing." *Mathematical Thinking and Learning,* 14 (4): 285–309.

Jilk, L. M. 2016. "Supporting Teacher Noticing of Students' Mathematical Strengths." *Mathematics Teacher Educator* 4 (2): 188–199.

Kalinec-Craig, C. 2017a. "Rights of the Learner: An Introduction." *Embracing Life with Major Revisions* (blog). https://embracinglifewithmajorrevisions.wordpress.com/2017/07/12/rights-of-the-learner-an-introduction/.

Kalinec-Craig, C. A. 2017b. "The Rights of the Learner: A Sociocultural Framework for Promoting Equity Through Formative Assessment in Mathematics Classrooms." *Democracy & Education* 25 (2): 5.

Kaplinsky, R. 2020. *Open Middle Math: Problems That Unlock Student Thinking, Grades 6–12.* Portsmouth, NH: Stenhouse.

Kelemanik, G., and A. Lucenta. 2019. "Contemplate Then Calculate." Fostering Math Practices. http://www.fosteringmathpractices.com/contemplate-then-calculate/.

Kelemanik, G., A. Lucenta, and S. J. Creighton. 2016. *Routines for Reasoning: Fostering the Mathematical Practices in All Students*. Portsmouth, NH: Heinemann.

Kilpatrick, J., J. Swafford, and B. Findell, eds. 2001. *Adding It Up: Helping Children Learn Mathematics*. Washington, DC: National Academies Press.

Lakatos, I. 1976. *Proofs and Refutations: The Logic of Mathematical Discovery*, ed. by J. Worrall and E. Zahar. New York: Cambridge University Press.

Lambert, R., P. Tan, J. Hunt, and A. Candela. 2018. "Rehumanizing the Mathematics Education of Students with Disabilities: Critical Perspectives on Research and Practice." *Investigations in Mathematics Learning* 10 (3): 129–132.

Lampert, M. 1990. "When the Problem Is Not the Question and the Solution Is Not the Answer: Mathematical Knowing and Teaching." *American Educational Research Journal* 27 (1): 29–63.

Lappan, G., Fey, J. T., Fitzgerald, W. M., Friel, S. N. and Phillips, E. D. 2002b. *Moving Straight Ahead*. Glenview, IL: Prentice Hall.

Leinwand, S., D. Brahier, D. Huinker, R. Berry, F. Dillon, M. Larson, M. Leiva, W. G. Martin, and M. S. Smith. 2014. *Principles to Actions: Ensuring Mathematical Success for All*. Reston, VA: National Council of Teachers of Mathematics.

Liljedahl, P. 2014. "The Affordances of Using Visually Random Groups in a Mathematics Classroom." In *Transforming Mathematics Instruction: Multiple Approaches and Practices*, ed. Y. Li, E. Silver, and S. Li (pp. 127–144). New York: Springer.

———. 2016. "Building Thinking Classrooms: Conditions for Problem-Solving." In *Posing and Solving Mathematical Problems* (pp. 361–386). Cham, Switzerland: Springer.

Mason, J., L. Burton, and K. Stacey. 2011. *Thinking Mathematically*. New York: Pearson Higher Ed.

Mathalicious. 2019. "Ice Cubed: What Size Ice Cubes Should You Put in Your Drink?" https://www.mathalicious.com/lessons/ice-cubed

Mathematics Assessment Resource Service. 2011. "Security Camera." Mathematics Assessment Project. https://www.map.mathshell.org/tasks.php?unit=HE01&collection=9.

Mercer, N., and S. Hodgkinson. 2008. *Exploring Talk in School: Inspired by the Work of Douglas Barnes*. London: Sage.

Meyer, D. 2010. "Math Class Needs a Makeover." TED video. https://www.ted.com/talks/dan_meyer_math_curriculum_makeover?language=en#t-402179.

My Favorite No: Learning from Mistakes. 2011. Teaching Channel video. https://www.teachingchannel.org/video/class-warm-up-routine.

National Council of Teachers of Mathematics. 2018. "Bobsled Sums." https://www.nctm.org/Classroom-Resources/Problems-of-the-Week/Bobsled-Sums/.

National Council of Teachers of Mathematics (NCTM). 2018. *Catalyzing Change in High School Mathematics: Initiating Critical Conversations*. Reston, VA: NCTM.

National Governors Association. 2010. "Common Core State Standards." Washington, DC. http://www.corestandards.org/Math/

Newell, C. 2017. "Precision over Perfection." YouTube video. https://youtu.be/wc3yU5YNpwE.

Newell, G. E. 2006. "Writing to Learn: How Alternative Theories of School Writing Account for Student Performance." In *Handbook of Writing Research*, ed. C. A. MacArthur, S. Graham, and J. Fitzgerald (pp. 235–247). New York: Guilford Press.

Nguyen, F. 2016. "7 Deadly Sins of Teaching [Maths]." *Finding Ways* (blog). http://fawnnguyen.com/7-deadly-sins-of-teaching-maths/.

Perry, M., and J. Lewis. 1999. "Verbal Imprecision as a Tool for Understanding Knowledge in Transition." *Developmental Psychology* 35 (3): 749–759.

Pólya, G. 1954. *Induction and Analogy in Mathematics*. Princeton, NJ: Princeton University Press.

Ray-Riek, M. 2011. "Why 2 > 4: A Proof by Induction." YouTube video. https://youtu.be/h00Ux1qx2zw.

———. 2013. *Powerful Problem Solving: Activities for Sense Making with the Mathematical Practices*. Portsmouth, NH: Heinemann.

Smith, M. S., E. K. Hughes, R. A. Engle, and M. K. Stein. 2009. "Orchestrating Discussions." *Mathematics Teaching in the Middle School* 14 (9): 548–556.

Smith, M. S., and M. G. Sherin. 2019. *The Five Practices in Practice: Successfully Orchestrating Mathematics Discussions in Your Middle School Classroom*. Thousand Oaks, CA: Corwin.

Stadel, A. 2012. "Estimation 180." http://www.estimation180.com/.

Statmore, E. 2014. "Talking Points Activity—Cultivating Exploratory Talk

Through a Growth Mindset Activity." *cheesemonkey wonders* (blog). http://cheesemonkeysf.blogspot.com/2014/07/tmc14-gwwg-talking-points-activity.html.

Thanheiser, E., and A. Jansen. 2016. "Inviting Prospective Teachers to Share Rough Draft Mathematical Thinking." *Mathematics Teacher Educator* 4 (2): 145–163.

VanDerWerf, S. 2016a. "Week 1 Day 1—Name Tents with Feedback." *VDW* (blog). https://www.saravanderwerf.com/week-1-day-1-name-tents-with-feedback/.

———. 2016b. "Number Talk Norms." In Number Talks presentation. PowerPoint slide, page 7. https://saravanderwerfdotcom.files.wordpress.com/2016/06/number-talks.pdf.

Von Glasersfeld, E., and L. P. Steffe. 1991. "Conceptual Models in Educational Research and Practice." *Journal of Educational Thought* 25 (2): 91–103.

Webel, C. 2010. "Shifting Mathematical Authority from Teacher to Community." *Mathematics Teacher* 104 (4): 315–318.

YouCubed. 2016. "Brains Grow and Change." Vimeo video. https://vimeo.com/177320916.

Zwiers, J., J. Dieckmann, S. Rutherford-Quach, V. Daro, R. Skarin, S. Weiss, and J. Malamut. 2017. *Principles for the Design of Mathematics Curricula: Promoting Language and Content Development.* Understanding Language/Stanford Center for Assessment, Learning and Equity. Stanford, CA: Stanford University Graduate School of Education. https://ell.stanford.edu/sites/default/files/u6232/ULSCALE_ToA_Principles_MLRs__Final_v2.0_030217.pdf.

index

K

L

M

N

O

P

S

T